Machine Learning for Experiment Design:
A Review, with a Focus on Active Learning

Jashan jii

Copyright © [2023]
Author: Jashan jii
Title : Machine Learning for Experiment Design:
A Review, with a Focus on Active Learning

All rights reserved. No part of this book may be reproduced or transmitted in any form or by any means, electronic or mechanical, including photocopying, recording, or by any information storage and retrieval system, without permission in writing from the author.

This book is a product of [**Publisher's Jashan jii**]

ISBN:

Table of Contents

1 Introduction   **1**
- 1.1 Background Information 1
  - 1.1.1 Machine Learning 1
  - 1.1.2 Active Learning 2
- 1.2 Problem and Current Popular Solution 3
- 1.3 Project Method and Goal 4
  - 1.3.1 Research Design 4
  - 1.3.2 Methods of the Alternative Approach 5
  - 1.3.3 Goal of the Project 6
  - 1.3.4 Delimitation 7
- 1.4 Outline 7

2 Background Theory   **8**
- 2.1 Kernel Density Estimation 8
- 2.2 Bayesian Optimization 9
- 2.3 Gaussian Processes 12
  - 2.3.1 Definition 12
  - 2.3.2 Posterior Calculation 12
  - 2.3.3 Kernel Function 13
- 2.4 Artificial Neural Networks 14
  - 2.4.1 A Neuron Model and a FNN Model 14
  - 2.4.2 Activation Function 15
  - 2.4.3 Training a FNN Model for Regression 17
- 2.5 Regression Tree Methods 17
  - 2.5.1 Regression Tree 18
  - 2.5.2 Bagging, Random Forests and Boosting 19

	2.6	Particle Swarm Optimization	20
	2.7	Tensor Flow Keras Sequential and Scikit-Learn	21

3 Toolbox Implementation — 22

    3.1 Data Preparation and Committee Initializing — 22
        3.1.1 Initialize Committee with Feedforward Neural Networks — 23
        3.1.2 Initialize Committee with Regression Trees — 24
        3.1.3 Initialize Committee with Other Models — 24
    3.2 Training Models from Committee — 25
        3.2.1 Interval Policy — 26
        3.2.2 Training Models in the Committee — 26
    3.3 Predict a x_next — 27
        3.3.1 Different Criteria of Expected Improvement Estimation — 28
        3.3.2 Running Average of EI — 30
        3.3.3 ϵ-mechanism — 30
    3.4 Other Methods for Prediction — 31
    3.5 Results Comparison and Function Generator — 33

4 Tests and Results — 35

    4.1 Test Examples — 35
        4.1.1 1D Example — 35
        4.1.2 2D Example — 37
        4.1.3 3D Example — 39
    4.2 Comparing GP with QBC in FNN Committee — 39
    4.3 Compare GP with QBC in RT Committee — 42
    4.4 Compare GP with QBC in GP Committee by Using Normal Distribution to Calculate EI — 43
    4.5 Compare GP with QBC in GP Committee by Using KDE to Calculate EI — 45
    4.6 Application in Industrial Simulation Problem — 46
        4.6.1 Settings and Further Explanations of the Experiment — 48
        4.6.2 Unpaced Flow Line with 6 Stations — 49
        4.6.3 Unpaced Flow Line with 9 Stations — 50
        4.6.4 Unpaced Flow Line with 12 Stations — 53

5 Analysis and Discussion — 56

    5.1 Toolbox Design and Implementation — 56
        5.1.1 Models in Committee — 56
        5.1.2 Stop Criteria and PSO Prediction Method — 57
    5.2 Comparison Experiments — 57
        5.2.1 Designs of the Experiments — 57
        5.2.2 Experiment Conclusions and Assumed Reasons — 58
    5.3 Application in Industrial Simulation Problem — 59

5.4 Future Work 60

6 Conclusion **61**

1 Introduction

1.1 Background Information

For many real world physical experiments, the cost of gaining a single sample is expensive, such as drilling cores from deep earth to obtain lithology information for oil and gas reservoir [1] or refining molecules for high-throughput compound screening in drug discovery [2]. For other experiments like software testing, selecting or generating samples in a proper size from a large number options is also time and cost demanding, such as creating samples for classifying hyperspectral images by convolutional neural network models [3], simulating autonomous driving validation with the visual rendering, physical simulation, and control agents [4]. Active Learning (AL) as a branch of machine learning is helpful under those situations and it is widely adopted (but not limited) in the field for designing experiments [5, 6].

1.1.1 Machine Learning

Machine learning partially begun from 1950s, and it evolved from many different aspects including interactions of brain cells, playing computer chess, image recognition, and even the traveling routes scheduling of a salesperson [7]. Machine learning is a research field focusing on the problem of how to build computer programs that improve their performances at some certain tasks through experience [8], or broadly speaking it is devoted to understanding and designing methods that make utmost use of data to improve performance when dealing with those tasks as part of artificial intelligence [9]. During the process, models will be built based on sample data, a.k.a. training data, to make predictions or decisions without being explicitly programmed to do so [9, 10].

Nowadays machine learning becomes the workhorse for big data technology, and it is applied and developed from researches on facial recognition, nature language processing, autonomous cars, medical treatment, e-commerce etc. [11, 12]. According to the types of the provided data, machine learning can be categorised into two main branches, supervised learning and unsupervised learning [12].

Supervised learning means that the model or prediction algorithm is developed from labeled data in pairs of observations, as (x_n, y_n) with $n = 1, 2, ..., N$. Here x_n is an vector being the input of the model, which is able to contain multiple variables a.k.a features, and the corresponding y_n is the desired (targeted) output, which can also be an vector contain many elements. The purpose is to obtain/estimate a functional relationship between x_n and y_n to predict the expected output value y for any given input x. The classic supervised learning is usually divided into the subfileds of classification and regression.

Unsupervised learning is the machine learning in data only having input variables but without label or output information. A common goal is to uncover the structure of the given data. Clustering, dimension reducing, probability distribution estimation and data generation are the branches of unsupervised learning. Figure 1.1 shows the work flow of supervised and unsupervised machine learning.

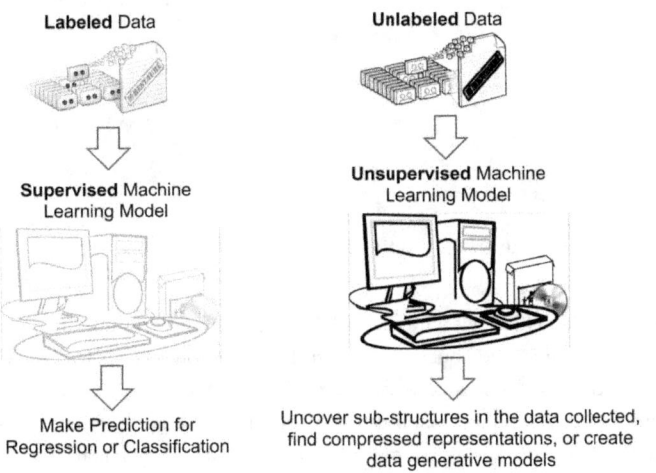

Figure 1.1: Supervised (left) and unsupervised (right) machine learning work flow

1.1.2 Active Learning

A proper number of labeled observations are necessary for achieving an acceptable estimate of a functional relationships between x_n and y_n when using supervised learning. Annotating instances by a person in a proper amount, such as rating 1 to 10 for watched movies or deciding pass or fail of a course for a class of students, does not seem to be difficult, but when it comes to scenarios as summarizing from an audio speech or classifying images in dozens categories, then manually performing those tasks will be tedious and expensive. Thus, algorithms with abilities to select data that truly contribute to its "learning" and perform well after learning from fewer data are desired.

An active learning method is designed as solutions for this, and it allows to interact with an oracle for querying labels of data where it learns, and selects the most informative data at each process step based on an user-assigned criteria/rule (like uncertainty and diversity) for achieving a good performance by using as few instances as possible [13].

Introduction

Active learning can be divided into different categories based on the query scenarios, and Figure 1.2 shows a general working process of active learning.

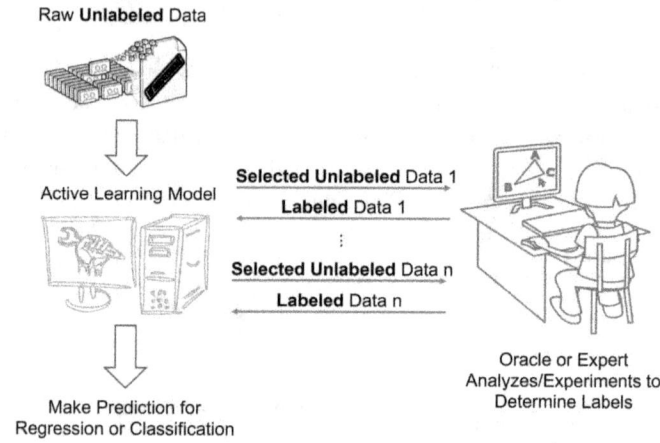

Figure 1.2: Active learning working process

Query By Committee (QBC) is a framework for data instance selection. In active learning, a committee is created and consists of multiple prediction models that are maintained and updated during process. The predicted label (which may be a discrete value or a real number) for a selected instance is determined based on somehow merging the votes/predictions of all committee members, and the candidate instance tested with the maximal disagreement on the votes/predictions is one common and intuitive choice used for the selection of the next instance sent to the oracle. [14]

Active learning is the study of machine learning systems that improve by asking questions [15]. Except the application in designing experiment as mentioned at the beginning, active learning is also used for filtering emails, articles or web pages for classification and filtering, annotating diseases mentioned in biomedical text for information extraction, and predicting and explaining the activity of proteins for computational biology [15].

Most of the application and research attentions in active learning are put on classification problems, although there are investigations applying it into regression and clustering [16, 17]. In this project, the focus is to apply active learning for regression in the context of global optimization of an unknown continuous valued function.

1.2 Problem and Current Popular Solution

Many problems from manufacturing production or computer science are essentially optimization problems, and usually those problems can be transformed into tasks as finding the optimum points of functions. However, many of the functions have many input variables and/or come without any concrete mathematical formula. Therefore, using a step-wise search method to gain the global optimum of those expensive or complicated functions by using as less steps/evaluations as possible to solve those problems is very desirable.

Active learning based global optimization can be implemented in many ways [6, 18–21], and Gaussian Processes (GPs) plays a popular and dominant role by being the surrogate of the underlying objective function in many suggested approaches. There are multiple reasons why GPs are commonly used in supervised learning. The first reason is from its attractive analytical properties. Gaussian Process based regression offers closed analytical expression for summation, conditioning and marginalization under certain basic criteria, and results are all in terms of Gaussian distributions. The second reason is the reducing of variables induces Occum's Razor automatically which can overcome overfitting issues [60]. The third reason is that Central Limit Theorem makes GPs suitable for many problems [61].

Although Gaussian process is a non-parametric model, the user specified kernel function and hyper-parameters as length scales pose huge influences on the predictive abilities, and optimization is usually needed for this part [62]. Meanwhile, there are also limitations of GPs, and they are (1) it demands high computation resources when inverting the kernel matrix; and (2) it is hard to find kernel functions to handle structured data [61]. But there are variants of GPs raised to overcome those limitations, such as Sparse Gaussian Processes for the computation and storage issues and Deep Gaussian Processes for hierarchical features extraction problem.

1.3 Project Method and Goal

1.3.1 Research Design

Gaussian Processes based regression along with its variants are used in a wide range [63], but they all require complicated theoretical knowledge in algebra and statistics. In order to try something simple and less theoretical, the project aims to investigate machine learning methods other than Gaussian Process based regression to be surrogate models for active learning (as an alternative approach) to solve the global optimization problems for unknown objective functions, then compare their performances over some functions to identify the advantages and disadvantages of different approaches, and last apply the most promising one for a production simulation scenario. However, GPs based regression modelling will also be implemented for comparing and investigating the pros and cons of those different approaches.

Therefore, the research questions of this thesis can be summarized as: How to use other machine learning methods other than GPs based regression within Active Learning

Introduction

framework to solve the global optimization problems for unknown objective functions? What is the performance of the investigated method compared with the classic GPs based regression over different type of functions and problems?

The project origins from a practical point of view, and based on the perspectives and the belief of knowledge development, the philosophy used in this project is positivism. The project is conducted under a deductive approach as a quantitative experiments. Because the desired alternative approach is developed under the basis of existed codes, functions, and frameworks etc., its performance is evaluated by comparing with the existed methods or algorithms, and conclusions are summarised from the statistics of the data that are presented in figures and tables. Secondary data and the non-probability sampling methods including convenience and snowball sampling are adopted.

1.3.2 Methods of the Alternative Approach

The general idea for solving the problem is to use supervised learning to iteratively improve the computation models used to estimate the hidden function of target problem. When using a GP method as a surrogate model for the unknown objective function to minimize, the uncertainty gained from the model will be used to guide the search towards the desired global optimum. In the alternative approaches studied here, QBC framework can be employed to obtain the uncertainty information for selecting next data point to query for a consensus model of the unknown objective function. Within this framework, multiple surrogate models can be gathered to build the committee, and multiple prediction response values for a single input then can be returned from the ensemble models during processing, which can be used for estimating the mean, variance and quantiles (a probability distribution) of an output.

When constructing the committee, different models, including polynomial fitting, Neural Networks, Regression Trees, and even Gaussian Process models, can be adopted or mixed. Supervised learning method is employed here as that all labeled observed data will be fed to the committee members for learning the hidden function.

When dealing with the global optimization problem, an assumed condition is that the true underlying function is expensive, the cost of gaining the label information of an instance is high, and the number of observed data is limited. With not enough training samples, it is not reliable by directly comparing the prediction responses from the committee members to gain the optimum minimum and then treat it as solution of the optimization problem, since the fitted models have a great chance in low prediction accuracy. Thus, using many deterministic prediction responses of the same x to estimate a probabilistic distribution of its true function value ($p(y|x)$) is a more convincing choice, because the true function value can be evaluated by the distribution with a probability.

In GPs, a Normal Probability Density Function (PDF) is returned directly, whereas by committee-based method, the PDF estimation is performed under the policy defined by the user, and different strategies can be used when estimate it. The assumption of prediction responses of an input being normally distributed, which is the same as the process in GPs, is one option. While Kernel Density Estimation (KDE) with its advantages of being able to estimated other kinds of distributions is another option here. By KDE method, the bandwidth can be chosen from rule-of-thumb or cross validation, and the number of committee members should be also considered since it directly decides the number of samples for the estimation inside KDE process.

After obtaining an estimated probability distribution of the function value for an input, Expected Improvement (EI) will be calculated and then used as the criterion to evaluate each instance. The candidate in maximum of EI will be selected as the next data for querying. In this project, the uncertainties of observed data for training the models in committee are set into zero, thus the EIs of theses points are all in zero, and the selected/query date will not be from the observed set. Once the label of a queried data is gained, this instance will be put into the observed group for training the models in the committee. The process is repeated (iterated) until a stop criteria is met.

The alternative approach is built on the framework of Query By Committee, therefore it will be referred as QBC in the following parts of the thesis if there is no extra explanation or reference.

In GPs, there are hyper-parameters related to Kernel function to control its tolerance of noise on the training observations. To test the stabilises of QBC, artificial data in different noise level with noise in a uniform distribution were generated by various functions (the true underlying functions) and then used for testing. Since the target problem is to find the vector x^* that leads to the optimum of the true underlying $f(x^*)$, the criteria for comparing QBC with GP is to count the number of steps/iterations/predictions to a x^* for gaining the optimum (minimum) of f, and method using less steps outperforms.

Based on those analysis and requirements, a flexible and development-friendly modular toolbox was built in Python in order to systematically evaluate the approach. It is compatible to multiple machine learning models for constructing various committees. Other features related to generate artificial data samples and compare among QBC, GP and random guess was also implemented in the toolbox.

1.3.3 Goal of the Project

There are many different machine learning models to be selected or mixed as a committee for query. To simplify the task and project, the ensembles of models acting as a committee are limited to ensemble Feedforward Neural Networks, ensemble Regression Trees, and ensemble Gaussian Process models.

Bases on the aims, methods and specified limitations, the goal of the project is detailed into the following five parts: (i) compare the performance of AL being done by using GP and by using QBC in FNNs; (Here "QBC in FNNs" means that the committee in QBC is built by multiple FNN models.) (ii) compare the performance of AL being done by using GP and by using QBC in RTs; (iii) compare the performance of AL being done by using GP and by using QBC in GPs with choosing normal distribution estimation to calculate EI; (iv) compare the performance of AL being done by GP and by using QBC in GPs with KDE to calculate EI; (v) implement the best performed QBA from (i) to (iv) into a practical industrial production simulation problem.

1.3.4 Delimitation

There are many machine learning algorithms involved in this project, and for each algorithm there are many parameters can be tuned to optimize its performance. Limited to the time and resource, only a few key parameters are controlled and investigated, and the choices of other parameters are set in default or by random within the existed framework.

1.4 Outline

The rest of this thesis is structured into five chapters. After a background theory introduction in chapter two, some implementation details of a toolbox based on the investigated approach are explained in chapter three. According to the discussed approach and its feature, test design and examples for using the toolbox over 1D, 2D and higher dimension functions are presented in Chapter four. Discussions and analysis in different aspects are presented in Chapter five, and conclusions are summarised in Chapter seven.

2 Background Theory

2.1 Kernel Density Estimation

KDE is a non-parametric statistical method to estimate the probability density function of a random variable based on a set of samples [22]. The essences of it is to better investigate the desired probability distribution other than using a traditional histogram [23].

Denote $\{x_1, x_2, \ldots, x_n\}$ is the independent and identically distributed sample of n observations drawn from an unknown density f at any given point x. The kernel density estimator $\hat{f}_h(x)$ of original $f(x)$ is defined as

$$\hat{f}(t) = \frac{1}{n} \sum_{i=1}^{n} K_i(x_i, t) \tag{2.1}$$

where $K(x,t)$ is the kernel function and non-negative for any real x,t. Having $\int_{-\infty}^{\infty} K(x,t)dt = 1$ for all real x, the normalization of the KDE in Funtion 2.1 is ensured by

$$\int_{-\infty}^{\infty} \hat{f}(t)dt = \frac{1}{n} \sum_{i=1}^{n} \int_{-\infty}^{\infty} K(x,t)dt = 1 \tag{2.2}$$

There are many choices/shapes for the kernel function, including uniform, triangular, Epanechnikov, Gaussian, Inverse Gaussian, Gamma, Lognormal and other distributions. But in most applications, the kernel estimation uses symmetric kernel function and because of the convenient mathematical properties, the normal kernel is often used. The symmetry leads to the kernel function in the most frequently used form as

$$K_{sym}(x,t) = \frac{1}{h} K\left(\frac{x-t}{h}\right) \tag{2.3}$$

where h is the smoothing parameter or bandwidth. When h is too small, too many insignificant details will be included in the estimator, while too large value of h will cause over-smoothing and mask some of important characteristics of $f(x)$. Many methods for fitting/estimating the smoothing parameter are available in literature, and the Rule-of-thumb method (Silverman's bandwidth [24]) is commonly used when the kernel is normal.

$$h = 0.9 \cdot min\left(\hat{\sigma}, \frac{IQR}{1.34}\right) \cdot n^{-\frac{1}{5}} \tag{2.4}$$

Here $\hat{\sigma}$ is standard deviation from the samples, IQR is the interquartile range, and n is the sample size.

2.2 Bayesian Optimization

Bayesian optimization (BO) is a common strategy for global optimization of functions that are usually expensive-to-compute or without detailed formula expression ("black-box function") [25]. There are two components of Bayesian optimization method. The first component is a probabilistic model $p(y|x)$ of the unknown objective function $F(x)$, and the second one is an acquisition function for deciding the next sampling point.

GPs are commonly used as the first component, but other techniques can be employed as well, including Parzen-Tree Estimator [26], polynomial regression, RT and ANN etc. [27]. Various acquisition functions can be defined and applied as the second component, such as Probability of Improvement [28], Upper Confidence Bound [29], Entropy [30] and Predictive Entropy [31] etc. EI [32] is also a well-known acquisition function, and the derivation of it in under different condition is as follows.

Denote $\hat{y}(x)$ is the prediction label of x, and y_{min} is the minimum observed value of the hidden objective function until now, then the predicted potential improvement $I(x)$ at a point x is defined as

$$I(x) = \begin{cases} y_{min} - \hat{y}(x), & if\ y_{min} > \hat{y}(x) \\ 0, & otherwise \end{cases} \tag{2.5}$$

Because the prediction $\hat{y}(x)$ is drawn from a distribution $p(\hat{y}|x)$ in BO, the average expected improvement in point x can be written as

$$I_{expected}(x) = E\{I|x\} = \int I(x)p(\hat{y}|x)d\hat{y} = \int_{-\infty}^{y_{min}} (y_{min} - \hat{y})p(\hat{y}|x)d\hat{y} \tag{2.6}$$

Different probabilistic models can be used to estimate $p(\hat{y}|x)$, and when a normal distribution with mean $\mu(x)$ and standard deviation $\sigma(x)$ is used, then Equation 2.6 can be further derived as

$$E\{I|x\} = I_{expected}(x) = \int_{-\infty}^{y_{min}} (y_{min} - \hat{y}) \frac{1}{\sigma\sqrt{2\pi}} e^{-\frac{1}{2}\left(\frac{\hat{y}-\mu}{\sigma}\right)^2} d\hat{y} \tag{2.7}$$

and a closed form can be gained after solving the integral, and the formula is as follows

$$E\{I|x\} = I_{expected}(x) = (y_{min} - \mu(x))\Phi(\frac{y_{min} - \mu(x)}{\sigma(x)}) + \sigma(x)\phi(\frac{y_{min} - \mu(x)}{\sigma(x)}) \quad (2.8)$$

Here $\Phi()$ and $\phi()$ are the cumulative distribution function and the PDF for the standard zero mean unit variance Gaussian distribution. The center gravity of the shadowed part in the following figure is the desired expected improvement.

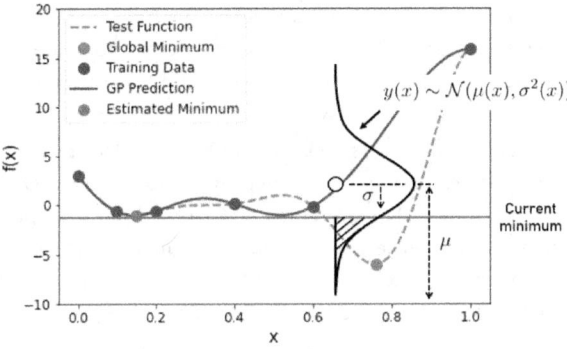

Figure 2.1: EI of a point when using Gaussian to estimate $p(\hat{y}|x)$ [18]

KDE can also be employed to estimate $p(\hat{y}|x)$. Suppose there are N predictions of $\hat{y}(x)$ in set $D = \{\hat{y}_1(x), \cdots, \hat{y}_N(x)\}$, $\hat{y}_n$ is the minimum in D, h is a specified standard deviation (the smoothing parameter/bandwidth in KDE), and normal kernels are used for KDE, then the estimated uncertainty for a given y of interest is as following

$$\hat{p}(y|D,h) = \frac{1}{N}\sum_{n=1}^{N} \frac{1}{h\sqrt{2\pi}} e^{-\frac{1}{2}(\frac{\hat{y}_n - y}{h})^2} \quad (2.9)$$

By this density function, the expected improvement in Equation 2.6 can be derived as

$$\begin{aligned} E\{I|x\} = I_{expected}(x) &= \int_{-\infty}^{y_{min}} (y_{min} - \hat{y}) \frac{1}{N}\sum_{n=1}^{N} \frac{1}{h\sqrt{2\pi}} e^{-\frac{1}{2}(\frac{\hat{y}_n - y}{h})^2} d\hat{y} \\ &= \frac{1}{N}\sum_{n=1}^{N} \underbrace{\int_{-\infty}^{y_{min}} (y_{min} - \hat{y}) \frac{1}{h\sqrt{2\pi}} e^{-\frac{1}{2}(\frac{\hat{y}_n - y}{h})^2} d\hat{y}}_{Q} \end{aligned} \quad (2.10)$$

and since normal kernels are used here, the integral part Q in Equation 2.10 can be derived by referencing Equation 2.8 in a closed form as following

$$Q = (y_{min} - \hat{y}_n)\Phi(\frac{y_{min} - \hat{y}_n}{h}) + h\phi(\frac{y_{min} - \hat{y}_n}{h}) \quad (2.11)$$

Background Theory

The workflow of the method is summarised as follows [25–27].

Step 1:	Create initial training examples from space-filling experiment to form an observed set;	
Step 2:	Fit parameters of the probabilistic model based on the observed set;	
Step 3:	For each possible candidate experiment x of interest, determine the uncertainty $p(y\|x)$ by means of the probabilistic model in Step 2;	
Step 4:	Select the instance that corresponds to optimum of the acquisition function and then determine its corresponding function value ;	
Step 5:	Extend the observed set by new training example created in Step 3;	
Step 6:	Repeat from Step 2 and Step 5 until meeting the stop criteria;	

The uncertainty in Step 3 can be obtained in multiple ways. One of them is by employing GP based Bayesian regression, which directly provides the desired PDF of $p(y|x)$ in the form of a Gaussian PDF. Another is to create a panel/committee of prediction models and then use their prediction responses $y_i(x)$ to estimate $p(y|x)$ as a Gaussian PDF or as a Kernel Density Estimator (average of Gaussians). An illustration of Bayesian optimization process is shown in the figure below [27].

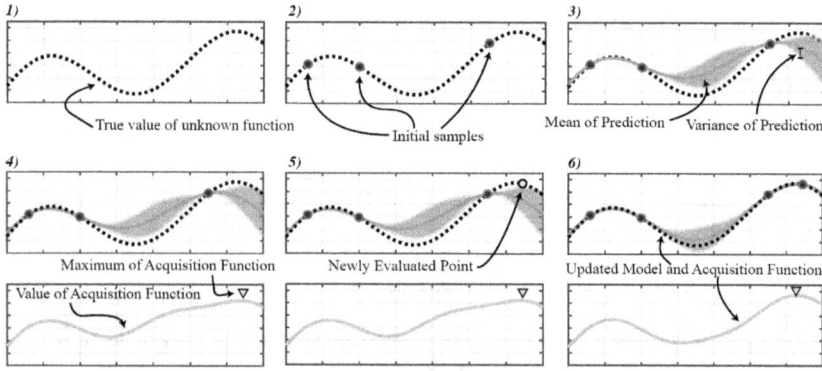

Figure 2.2: Work process of Bayesian optimization [27]

(1) Showing the true underlying function used for illustrating the process of BO; (2) Gaining the initial sampling points within the given range randomly (Step 1); (3) Building/Fitting a probabilistic model of the function based on the samples, and returning a mean prediction value along with a variance of the prediction at every point in the region (Step 2 and 3); (4) Evaluating each candidate point of interest by acquisition function (Step 4); (5) Selecting the candidate point leading to the maximum acquisition function value and determining its true underlying function value to extend the observed set (Step 4 and 5); (6) Updating the probabilistic model and the acquisition function evaluation by the extended observed set (Step 6);

2.3 Gaussian Processes

2.3.1 Definition

A Gaussian Process is a special type of stochastic process, indexed by time and space where every finite subsampling of values is multivariate normally distributed [33, 34].

2.3.2 Posterior Calculation

Let $\mathcal{X}$ be the input space, $f : \mathcal{X} \to R$ be a function from the input domain to the reals, and $k : \mathcal{X}, \mathcal{X} \to R$ with any $k(\mathbf{x}_i, \mathbf{x}_j) = k(\mathbf{x}_j, \mathbf{x}_i)$ be the covariance/kernel function. When given an observed data set $((\mathbf{x}_1, f(\mathbf{x}_1)), (\mathbf{x}_2, f(\mathbf{x}_2)), ..., (\mathbf{x}_n, f(\mathbf{x}_n)))$ as $(\mathbf{X}, f(\mathbf{X}))$ in pairs, and a Gaussian process prior on f with mean function as $\mu(\mathbf{X})$ and covariance function as $\mathbf{K}(\mathbf{X}, \mathbf{X}))$, then for any query input $\mathbf{x}^*$, a joint distribution can be written as

$$p\left(\begin{bmatrix} f(\mathbf{x}^*) \\ f(\mathbf{X}) \end{bmatrix}\right) = N\left(\begin{bmatrix} f(\mathbf{x}^*) \\ f(\mathbf{X}) \end{bmatrix}; \begin{bmatrix} \mu(\mathbf{x}^*) \\ \mu(\mathbf{X}) \end{bmatrix}, \begin{bmatrix} k(\mathbf{x}^*, \mathbf{x}^*) & \mathbf{K}(\mathbf{x}^*, \mathbf{X}) \\ \mathbf{K}(\mathbf{X}, \mathbf{x}^*) & \mathbf{K}(\mathbf{X}, \mathbf{X}) \end{bmatrix}\right)$$

and the conditional probability distribution of $f(\mathbf{x}^*)$ given $f(\mathbf{X})$ can be derived as

$$p(f(\mathbf{x}^*)|f(\mathbf{X})) = N(f(\mathbf{x}^*); \mu^*, \Sigma^*)$$
$$\mu^* = \mu(\mathbf{x}^*) + \mathbf{K}(\mathbf{X}, \mathbf{x}^*)^T \mathbf{K}(\mathbf{X}, \mathbf{X})^{-1}(f(\mathbf{X}) - \mu(\mathbf{X})) \quad (2.12)$$
$$\Sigma^* = k(\mathbf{x}^*, \mathbf{x}^*) - \mathbf{K}(\mathbf{X}, \mathbf{x}^*)^T \mathbf{K}(\mathbf{X}, \mathbf{X})^{-1} \mathbf{K}(\mathbf{X}, \mathbf{x}^*)$$

with μ^* and Σ^* as the mean and covariance matrix of a normal distribution. In most applications, the prior mean function is set into zero for simplifying the calculation. Notably the mean of the posterior (μ^* from Equation 2.12) usually is not zero although the prior has a zero mean.

When additive noise is present for example so that the observed data are $y(\mathbf{x}) = f(\mathbf{x}) + \epsilon$ with $\epsilon \sim N(0, \alpha^2)$, then the joint distribution can be written as

$$p\left(\begin{bmatrix} f(\mathbf{x}^*) \\ y(\mathbf{X}) \end{bmatrix}\right) = N\left(\begin{bmatrix} f(\mathbf{x}^*) \\ y(\mathbf{X}) \end{bmatrix}; \begin{bmatrix} \mu^* \\ \mu(\mathbf{X}) \end{bmatrix}, \begin{bmatrix} k(\mathbf{x}^*, \mathbf{x}^*) + \alpha^2 & \mathbf{K}(\mathbf{x}^*, \mathbf{X}) \\ \mathbf{K}(\mathbf{X}, \mathbf{x}^*) & \mathbf{K}(\mathbf{X}, \mathbf{X}) + \alpha^2 \mathbf{I} \end{bmatrix}\right)$$

The only difference compared with the noise-free case is that the covariance matrix here adds an σ^2 term on the diagonal. The reason is that the noise is independent from both the observations and f. Based on this, the posterior on $f(\mathbf{x}^*)$ can be derived and written as

$$p(f(\mathbf{x}^*)|y(\mathbf{X})) = N(f(\mathbf{x}^*); \mu_n^*, \Sigma_n^*)$$
$$\mu_n^* = \mu(\mathbf{x}^*) + \mathbf{K}(\mathbf{X}, \mathbf{x}^*)^T (\mathbf{K}(\mathbf{X}, \mathbf{X}) + \sigma^2 \mathbf{I})^{-1} (y(\mathbf{X}) - \mu(\mathbf{X})) \quad (2.13)$$
$$\Sigma_n^* = k(\mathbf{x}^*, \mathbf{x}^*) - \mathbf{K}(\mathbf{X}, \mathbf{x}^*)^T (\mathbf{K}(\mathbf{X}, \mathbf{X}) + \sigma^2 \mathbf{I})^{-1} \mathbf{K}(\mathbf{X}, \mathbf{x}^*)$$

2.3.3 Kernel Function

When using GPs for supervised learning, once can do both regression and classification for applications such as motion planning to finds optimal trajectories for robotics [35] and historical Chinese character recognition [36]. A vital factor influencing the performance is the choice of kernel function, since it decides the similarities between two data points. When two kernel function values $k(\mathbf{x}_i, \mathbf{x}_j)$ and $k(\mathbf{x}_i, \mathbf{x}_k)$ have $k(\mathbf{x}_i, \mathbf{x}_j) > k(\mathbf{x}_i, \mathbf{x}_k)$, then $\mathbf{x}_i$ is considered to be closer to $\mathbf{x}_j$ than to $\mathbf{x}_k$ [33].

There are various kernel functions, such as Linear Kernel ($k(\mathbf{x}_i, \mathbf{x}_j) = \mathbf{x}_i^T \mathbf{x}_j$), Polynomial Kernel ($k(\mathbf{x}_i, \mathbf{x}_j) = (c + \mathbf{x}_i^T \mathbf{x}_j)^{d-1}$), and Sigmoid Kernel ($k(\mathbf{x}_i, \mathbf{x}_j) = tanh\left(a\mathbf{x}_i^T \mathbf{x}_j + b\right)$) etc., encoded with different assumptions on application situations or the models. Squared Exponential Kernel ($k(x_i, x_j) = exp(-\frac{(x_i - x_j)^2}{2l^2})$), is applied under the assumption of the objective function being smooth, and a high kernel function value should be returned when two points being nearby in parameter space, but a small value when they are far away.

More complicate kernels can be constructed by adding different kernels together or multiplying a positive number (α^2) before a kernel function. Meanwhile, there are usually hyper-parameters like the a, b, c, d, l, α^2 in the named Kernel functions. The method of tuning those parameters is usually to maximize the marginal likelihood $p(y(\mathbf{X})|D)$ (D is the observation data set with N instances). When putting all parameters into one vector η, the values of η yielding the max value of function in Equation 2.14 contains the optimized hyper-parameters. [33]

$$\ln\left(p(y(\mathbf{X})|D, \eta\right) = \ln\left(\mathcal{N}(y(\mathbf{X}); \mu(\mathbf{X}), \mathbf{K}_\eta(\mathbf{X}, \mathbf{X}))\right) = \ln\left(\frac{1}{\sqrt{(2\pi)^N |\Sigma|}} e^{-\frac{1}{2}(\mathbf{X}-\mu)^T \Sigma^{-1}(\mathbf{X}-\mu)}\right)$$

$$= -\frac{1}{2} y(\mathbf{X})^T \left(\mathbf{K}(\mathbf{X}, \mathbf{X}) + \sigma^2 \mathbf{I}\right)^{-1} y(\mathbf{X}) - \frac{1}{2} \ln(det(\mathbf{K}(\mathbf{X}, \mathbf{X}) + \sigma^2 \mathbf{I})) - \frac{N}{2} \ln(2\pi) \quad (2.14)$$

Meanwhile attentions should be paid to the initial guess of the hyper parameters, since there might be several optimum solutions for Equation 2.14. Also, the computation complexity is increased exponentially ($\mathcal{O}(N^3)$ for optimizing η) due to the determinant and inverse calculation of the covariance matrix when the number of observations increases.

GPs have been applied successfully in many cases including interpolation for generating geoinforamtion, forecasting stock prices, energy consumptions etc. [37, 38] for regression, image recognition [39], infrastructure damage assessment [40], and industrial processes [41] etc. for classification.

2.4 Artificial Neural Networks

The development of Artificial Neural Networks has a long history after the combining neurophysiology with mathematical logic and creating the perceptron Learning Algorithm [42–44]. There are many different architectures for ANN models nowadays, such as Convolutional Neural Networks and Recurrent Neural Networks etc., but here focus will be put on the simplest Feedforward Neural Network (FNN) models [44].

2.4.1 A Neuron Model and a FNN Model

FNN model begins with an input layer and ends up with an output layer, and between them there might be zero or many hidden layers. The basic element of a layer (expect the input layer) is a single neuron model, a.k.a. node. The typical characteristic of a FNN is that the information within the model only flows forward from input to output layer due to the full connections between a node and its previous layer and there being no cycle among those connections [44].

The structure of a node is shown in Figure 2.3. The scalars $x_1, x_2, x_3, \ldots, x_n$ are variables from input layer or outputs from the (hidden) layer just before the node, and the scalar y is the output. The neuron will first perform a sum based on the weights $w_1, w_2, w_3, \ldots, w_n$ from each connection and the offset item b from itself, and then use an activation function denoted f to generate a output as $y = f(b + \sum_{i=1}^{n} w_i x_i)$. The y here is as a prediction if the neuron is in the output layer, otherwise as a input for the nodes in next layer.

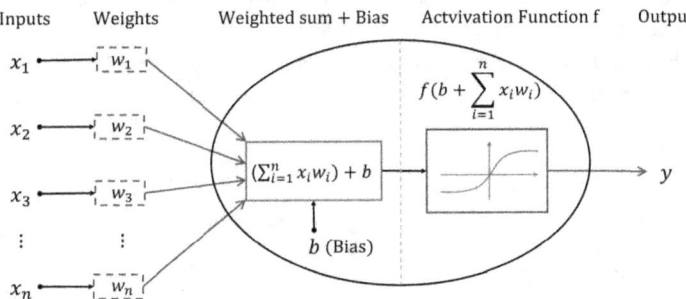

Figure 2.3: An artificial neuron model for FNN

On this basis, a simple example to illustrate a FNN model structure is shown in Figure 2.4. There are a input layer with four input variables, two hidden layers with each having three nodes, and an output layer with one node. The dimension of input layer should be the same as the input dimension of an observed instance, and the values of variables from the instance will be used as inputs directly for next layer without weighted sum and activation function process. The number of neurons in output layer should be the dimension of the output of an observed instance for regression problem,

Background Theory

and for classification problem, it should be the number of classes. However, the number of nodes in each hidden layer is able to be user-specified, and in convention a layer closer to input layer is supposed to have equal or more neurons than layers after it.

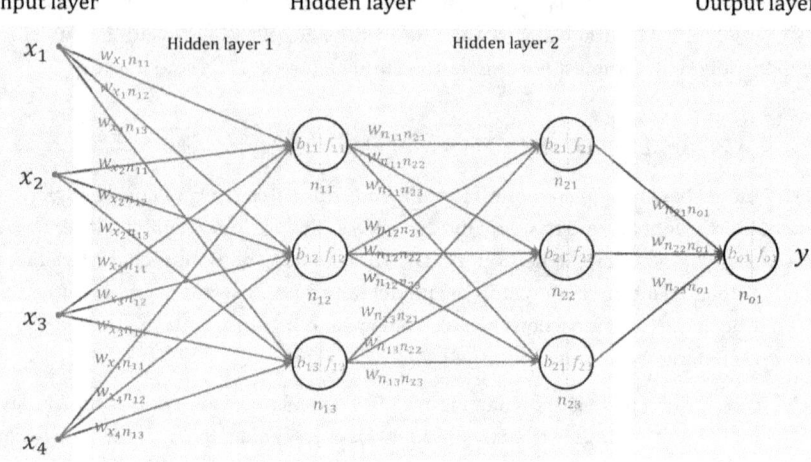

Figure 2.4: A FNN model structure

Based on the above description, all the required weights, biases, and activation functions of the example FNN model are named and marked in Figure 2.4. Denote n_{12} is the second neuron in the first hidden layer, b_{12} is its bias, f_{12} is its activation function, $y_{n_{12}}$ is its output, and $w_{x_1 n_{12}}$ is the weight for the connection between input variable x_1 and n_{12}, then the relation for the input $(x_1, x_2, x_3, \ldots, x_n)$ and output (y) of an instance can be derived by following functions

$$
\begin{aligned}
&(1)\ y_{n_{11}} = f_{11}\left(b_{11} + \sum_{i=1}^{4} x_i w_{x_i n_{11}}\right) &&(5)\ y_{n_{22}} = f_{22}\left(b_{22} + \sum_{i=1}^{3} y_{n_{1i}} w_{n_{1i} n_{22}}\right) \\
&(2)\ y_{n_{12}} = f_{12}\left(b_{12} + \sum_{i=1}^{4} x_i w_{x_i n_{12}}\right) &&(6)\ y_{n_{23}} = f_{23}\left(b_{23} + \sum_{i=1}^{3} y_{n_{1i}} w_{n_{1i} n_{23}}\right) \\
&(3)\ y_{n_{13}} = f_{13}\left(b_{13} + \sum_{i=1}^{4} x_i w_{x_i n_{13}}\right) &&(7)\ y_{n_{o1}} = f_{o1}\left(b_{o1} + \sum_{i=1}^{3} y_{n_{2i}} w_{n_{2i} n_{o1}}\right) \\
&(4)\ y_{n_{21}} = f_{21}\left(b_{21} + \sum_{i=1}^{3} y_{n_{1i}} w_{n_{1i} n_{21}}\right) &&(8)\ y = y_{n_{o1}}
\end{aligned}
\quad (2.15)
$$

2.4.2 Activation Function

The relations among the functions in Equation 2.15 shows that if there is no activation function in a FNN model, then the whole network is performing linear regression, and nonlinear relations between the input and output of an instance cannot be learned. Therefore, the activation function is vital part for FNN models, and the commonly used ones are summarized in the table below [45, 46].

Function	Plot	A General Summary
Binary $f(x) = \begin{cases} 1, x \geq 0 \\ 0, x < 0 \end{cases}$		Can only output 1 or 0 thus cannot be used for situations with multiple outputs; Hindrance in the back-propagation process due to the gradient of the step function being zero;
Linear $f(x) = x$		Usually used in output layer;
Tanh $f(x) = \frac{1-e^{-2x}}{1+e^{-2x}}$		Output is between -1 and 1 with center at 0 thus able to map output in negative, neutral or positive; Usually used in hidden layer; Smooth gradient for x from $-\infty$ to ∞, but close to 0 when x is large; That leads to difficulties for updating the network when training;
Sigmoid $f(x) = \frac{1}{1+e^{-x}}$		Output ranges from 0 to 1, thus usually used for situations with probability as the output. Smooth gradient for x from $-\infty$ to ∞, but close to 0 when x is large; That leads to difficulties for updating the network when training;
ReLU $f(x) = \begin{cases} x, x \geq 0 \\ 0, x < 0 \end{cases}$		Most popular choice; Neuron will not be activated if the linear transformation is negative since it is 0 when $x < 0$; Gradient in 0 when $x < 0$ and may cause dead neuron (Dying ReLU);

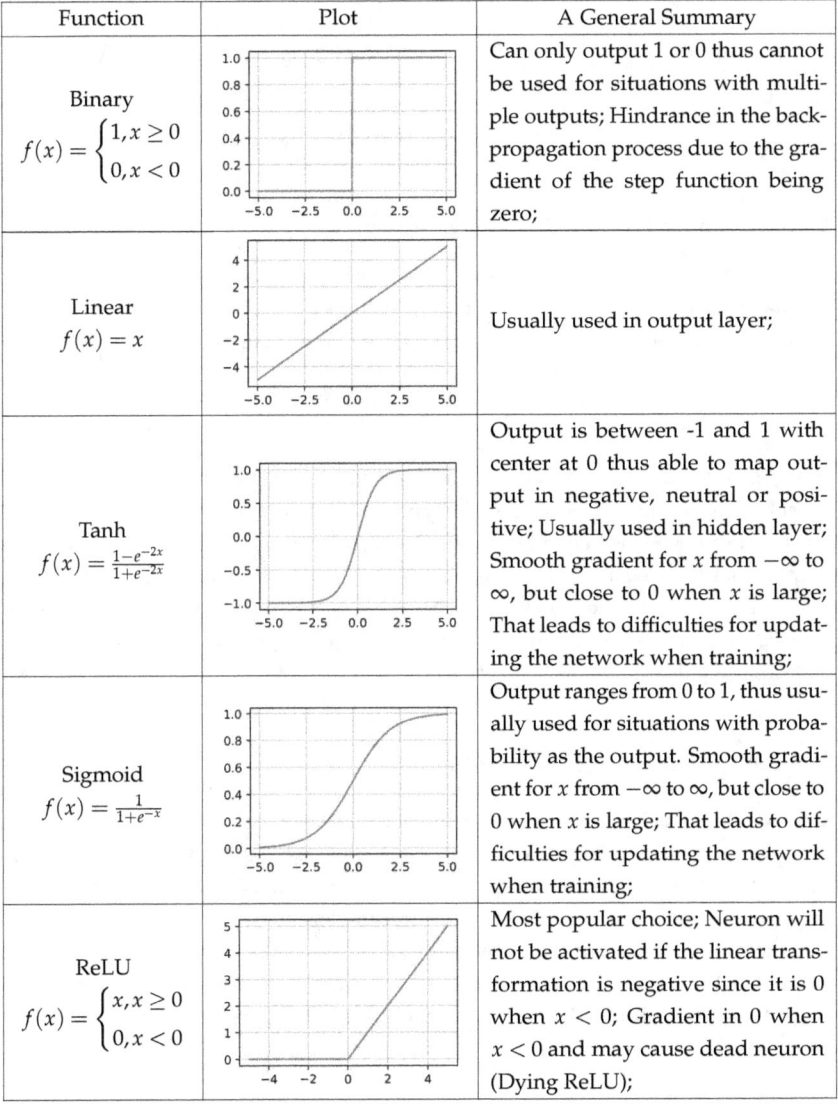

Table 2.1: Common used activation functions continue...

Function	Plot	A General Summary
PReLU $f(x) = \begin{cases} x, x \geq 0 \\ \alpha x, x < 0 \end{cases}$	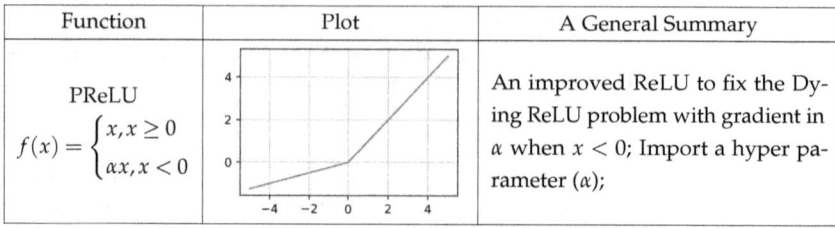	An improved ReLU to fix the Dying ReLU problem with gradient in α when $x < 0$; Import a hyper parameter (α);

Table 2.1: Common used activation functions

2.4.3 Training a FNN Model for Regression

The core idea for a FNN model "learning" from the given data is to find out the proper parameters (θ) including the weight matrix (**W**) for all the connections and bias vectors (**V**) for all neurons in the network by solving the following optimization problem.

$$\hat{\theta} = \underset{\theta}{\mathrm{argmin}}\ \mathbf{J}(\theta),\ where\ \mathbf{J}(\theta) = \frac{1}{n}\sum_{i=1}^{n}\mathbf{L}(x_i, y_i, \theta) \qquad (2.16)$$

Here $\mathbf{J}(\theta)$ is the cost function, and $\mathbf{L}(x_i, y_i, \theta)$ is the loss function. Different forms of loss function will be used depending on the types of a problem. For regression task, Mean Squared Error (MSE) is frequently used as $\mathbf{L}(x, y, \theta) = (y - f(x, \theta))^2$ with $f(x, \theta)$ as the output of a FNN model. The updating processes of the parameters is usually performed under an iterative manner by using gradient based search method, and the steps are (i) initializing θ in θ_0, (ii) updating parameters to θ_{t+1} by $\theta_t - \gamma \nabla_\theta \mathbf{J}(\theta_t)$ for $t = 0, 1, 2, ...$, and (iii) using θ_t as $\hat{\theta}$ when termination criteria is met. [33]

2.5 Regression Tree Methods

Decision tree is able to efficiently process large dataset, and it is capable of solving classification or regression problems [47]. The method constructs an inverted tree model by dividing the input and output spaces of observations into different disjoint segments through root, internal and leaf nodes [33]. Tree models with output/target variables in discrete values are classification trees, in which the leave nodes are for class labels and the root and internal nodes are conjunct features leading to the class labels; When the output/target variables take continuous values as real numbers, then the tree models are regression trees [48].

2.5.1 Regression Tree

The first regression tree algorithm was published for Automatic Interaction Detection [49], but the instrumental Classification And Regression Trees (CART) algorithm [50] for regression problem will be partially introduced here.

Denote the observations data set T is $\{(x_1,y_1),(x_2,y_2),\ldots,(x_n,y_n)\}$ containing n points with x_i as a vector $[x_{i1}, x_{i2},\ldots, x_{im}]$ having m variables and y_i as a variable for $i = 1,2,\ldots,n$, and $\hat{y}_*$ is the response/prediction when feed x_* into the model. Suppose there are L regions (leaf nodes at the bottom level), and R_l as the lth region returns a constant C_l (a numerical variable for regression) as prediction. Then regression tree model can be defined as a piecewise constant function over the input x_* as:

$$\hat{y}_* = \sum_{l=1}^{L} C_l \mathbb{I}\{x_l \in R_l\} \tag{2.17}$$

with indicator function $\mathbb{I}\{x_l \in R_l\} = 1$ if $x_l \in R_l$, and $\mathbb{I}\{x_l \in R_l\} = 0$ otherwise.[33]

Building a proper regression tree according to data set T is to find out suitable values of L and $\{C_1, C_2,\ldots, C_L\}$. If minimising the sum of squared errors ($\sum_{i=1}^{n}(\hat{y}_i - y_i)^2$) is chosen as the termination criteria, then it is easy to conclude that for any C_l in $\{C_1, C_2,\ldots, C_L\}$

$$C_l = Average\{y_i : x_i \in R_l \text{ for } i = 1,2,\ldots,n\} \tag{2.18}$$

is solution of the minimising problem. While for the tree size L, the basic solution is to select regions that fit all the outputs in T, but a computational infeasibility will be caused by the explosion of combinations when binary partitioning input space for a minimum sum of squares [51]. Therefore, the greedy algorithm, recursive binary splitting that is only focusing on the current split at a time and then deciding the splitting rule from root to leaf nodes one after one, is used to find out L. Starting from the root node, consider a splitting variable j from the m variables and a cutpoint s for $\{x_{1j}, x_{2j},\ldots, x_{nj}\}$, the input space can be divided into 2 half-planes

$$R_1(j,s) = \{x : x_j < s\} \quad and \quad R_2(j,s) = \{x : x_j \geq s\} \tag{2.19}$$

and j, s should be decided by

$$j,s = \underset{j,s}{argmin} \left\{ \underset{C_1}{argmin} \sum_{x_i \in R_1(j,s)} (y_i - C_1)^2 + \underset{C_2}{argmin} \sum_{x_i \in R_2(j,s)} (y_i - C_2)^2 \right\} \tag{2.20}$$

The inner squared terms is a commonly used loss function, sum of squared error, and the minimise problem of this loss function can be solved by

$$\hat{C}_1 = Average\{y_i : x_i \in R_1(j,s)\} \quad and \quad \hat{C}_2 = Average\{y_i : x_i \in R_2(j,s)\} \tag{2.21}$$

Other loss functions can also be used here, but the inner *argmin* solution will be different from that in 2.21. [33, 51]

The splitting point s can be quickly gained by this way and hence the best pair (j,s) can be determined after going through all the m input variables. After that, fix the splitting rule on this level and repeat the processes in its left and right branch for further constructing the tree. Obviously the tree can grow regions/leaves with each only contains a training data point ($L = n$) if there is no stopping criteria, and that the fully grown tree predicting correctly on each training data point leads high risks on overfitting. Thus early termination criteria such as the maximum depth of the tree and minimum number of data points on a leaf node, or pruning methods based on weakest-link cutting to minimise cost complexity are supposed to be applied when construct a tree. [33, 51, 52]

2.5.2 Bagging, Random Forests and Boosting

Bootstrapping is a method to generate multiple datasets from one given dataset (T) and all those sets contain the same amount of data (in size n). The process is to sample with replacement n times from T and group the samples as a new dataset, and repeat these two steps multiple times to have the desired number (B) of new datasets. The bootstrapped datasets on average contain only 63% unique examples from T, and a set may contain many copies of a data point in T while some other points in T might not be included at all. [33]

An ensemble method combines multiple instances of basic models to gain "wisdom of crowds" by obtaining a final prediction through a (possibly weighted) average or majority vote after each base model making its own prediction.

Bootstrap aggregating or bagging is an ensemble method. Each base model in bagging is constructed the same way except that its the training data is the bootstrapped one of the provided data, and with the models being weighted equally.

Random forests is a bagging method but only uses classification or regression trees as its base model. The number of the selected variables q at each tree node is a hyper parameter. Suppose there are p variables, then a common choices are that $q = \sqrt{p}$ for classification problem and $q = \frac{p}{3}$ for regression problem.

Boosting is another ensemble method and aims at reducing bias by grouping ensemble weak models (such as a classification tree of one depth) into a strong one. In bagging, the base models are parallel and can be built simultaneously; But in boosting, the ensemble models are constructed sequentially. The training data for an individual model in boosting will be put into different weights to focus on the ones that the already-existed models poorly performed on, and every model is built to correct the mistakes made by the previous model. The final output from boosting is based on a weighted average or a weighted majority vote from all base models. The first successfully implemented boosting methods is AdaBoost (Adaptive Boosting) algorithm, while the more modern approach is Gradient Boosting.

2.6 Particle Swarm Optimization

Particle Swarm Optimization (PSO) as a computational method is discovered through simulation of a simplified social model [53], and it usually deals with the following minimum-optimizing problem [54] by iteratively attempting to improve a candidate solution with regard to a specified measure of quality [55].

$$find \ \vec{x} \in S \subset \mathbb{R}^d \ such \ that \ \forall \vec{y} \in S, \ f(\vec{x}) \leq f(\vec{y}) \tag{2.22}$$

Inside the problem 2.22, S is the search space with $\{\vec{y}: l_i \leq y_i \leq u_i\}$, y_i is the ith dimension of vector $\vec{y}$, l_i and u_i are the lower and upper limit of the ith dimension, d is the total number of dimensions, and f is the objective function.

PSO is a population (referred as the swarm inside the name) based approach and contains no less than one particle. Each particle is defined by three d-dimensional vectors, that are Position ($\vec{x}_t^i$), Velocity ($\vec{v}_t^i$) and Personal Best ($\vec{p}_t^i$) vectors. $\vec{x}_t^i$ determines the quality of a particle, and it is the position of ith particle in tth iteration. $\vec{v}_t^i$ is the movement length and direction of ith particle in tth iteration, and it is usually constrained within a specified limit. $\vec{p}_t^i$ is the best position that the ith particle has visited in its lifetime till the tth iteration, and it is the memory that stores the the location of highest quality solutions found by this particle so far.

Standard PSO [54] will be briefly introduced and used in this project. Within it there is a Global Best vector $\vec{g}_t$ that contains the best position of the whole swarm found so far, and it is the $\vec{p}_t^j$ with $f(\vec{p}_t^j)$ being the optimum minimum when $j = 1, \ldots, n$ (n is the number of particles) after t iterations.

The Position ($\vec{x}_t^i$), Velocity ($\vec{v}_t^i$) and Personal Best ($\vec{p}_t^i$) vectors of each particle in the swarm will be updated at every iteration by the following schema

$$\begin{aligned}
\vec{v}_{t+1}^i &= w\vec{v}_t^i + w_1 R_{1t}^i (\vec{p}_t^i - \vec{x}_t^i) + w_2 R_{2t}^i (\vec{g}_t - \vec{x}_t^i) \\
\vec{x}_{t+1}^i &= \vec{x}_t^i + \vec{v}_{t+1}^i \\
\vec{p}_{t+1}^i &= \begin{cases} \vec{x}_{t+1}^i, & if \ f(\vec{x}_{t+1}^i) < f(\vec{p}_t^i) \ and \ \vec{x}_{t+1}^i \in S \\ \vec{p}_t^i, & otherwise \end{cases}
\end{aligned} \tag{2.23}$$

The i in the above functions will be from 1 to n, and the Global Best vector will also be updated after each iteration. Within the updated function for $\vec{v}_{t+1}^i$, w, w_1, w_2 are the inertia, cognitive and social weight respectively, $\vec{p}_t^i - \vec{x}_t^i$ is the cognitive influence factor, $\vec{g}_t - \vec{x}_t^i$ is the social influence factor, R_{1t}^i and R_{2t}^i are two $d \times d$ diagonal matrices with their elements are random numbers from the uniform distribution in [0, 1], and they are generated for each particle in each iteration independently.

The updating process of those vectors, or the process of finding the optimum minimum will be stopped until it reaches a predefined stopping criteria, such as maximum number of iterations and a sufficiently good objective value being found. The final Global Best vector will be the final output solution as the desired optimum minimum point.

2.7 Tensor Flow Keras Sequential and Scikit-Learn

Tensor Flow is an end-to-end open source machine learning platform, it is free and flexible to be used in various programming languages including the most notably Python, as well as Javascript, C++, and Java. TensorFlow is developed by the Google Brain team, and able to deal with across a range of tasks but has a special focus on training and inference of deep neural networks. Based on the platform of TensorFlow, Keras is developed with a focus on enabling fast experimentation as a deep learning API written in Python. A Sequential model in Keras is appropriate for a plain stack of layers where each layer has exactly one input tensor and one output tensor when constructing Artificial Neural Network models. [56, 57]

Scikit-learn, a.k.a sklearn, is a free and open-source software machine learning library for the Python programming language, and it is simple and efficient tools for predictive data analysis. The software contains features to solve classification, regression and clustering problems, and algorithms including random forests, Gaussian Process, and k-means etc are built-in inside it. Sicikt-learn is built on the Python numerical and scientific libraries NumPy and SciPy, and visualised by matplotlib library. [58, 59]

3 Toolbox Implementation

The designed workflow of the toolbox is as follows. Based on these steps, the structure of the toolbox is able to be grouped into three parts, and they are initialized to create the committee (Step 2 to 3), fitting the models in the committee to make predictions (Step 4 to 7), and predicting by other methods to compare the results (Step 8 and 9).

Step 1:	Prepare the dataset for training and prediction
Step 2:	For i in 1, 2, 3, ..., N:
	Define model i
	Put model i into the committee
Step 3:	For model i from model 1, 2, 3, ..., N:
	Fit model i with the training dataset
Step 4:	For model i from model 1, 2, 3, ..., N:
	Use model i to make predictions over the given x_range
	Gather all the predictions into one array
Step 5:	Calculate the mean and variance of the predictions for each point
	Use a user designed method to calculate the EI for each point
Step 6:	Find out the point with the maximum EI as the prediction of x_next
Step 7:	If predict multiple steps:
	Put x_next and its corresponding y into the training dataset
	Repeat Step 3 to Step 6 the asked times
Step 8:	Use Gaussian Process/Random Guess/PSO to predict x_next if needed
Step 9:	Count the steps of having the optimum for each used method

The toolbox only works for global optimization, and the prediction in Step 4 means that a model returns a function value (y) for a given input (x), while in Step 6 and Step 8 it means that the tool returns a x as the expected position to have the optimum y value over the whole search space. Based on the structures and features, five subsections are presented for a detailed introduction.

3.1 Data Preparation and Committee Initializing

The search space information and the training dataset are necessary for the tool to make a prediction of *x_next*. The query committee is flexible to contain many models in

Toolbox Implementation

different types, but the type and the initializing parameters of each model are required to be specified when initializing. The general step of building a committee is to create a model and then put it into the committee as a member.

To simulate the realistic situation, noise is added to the original simulated data set. Different noise levels are used to generate data because of the necessity for performance testing. The formulas for generating y_{noise} from the search space x with the original function f are the following:

$$y_{noise\_free} = f(x)$$
$$Noise\_distance = Noise\_level \cdot Max\_distance\_among\_y \qquad (3.1)$$
$$y_{noise} = y_{noise\_free} + Uniform(-1,1) \cdot Noise\_distance$$

The **Uniform(-1, 1)** is for generating a random number from the uniform distribution in interval [-1, 1], and it makes y_{noise} able to be "up" and "down" side of y_{noise_free}. *Noise_level* is a percentage in $[0,1]$ to indicate the noise level. *Max_distance_among_y* is the maximum L2 distance among all y_{noise_free} data, thus in 1D case it is $max(y_{noise\_free}) - min(y_{noise\_free})$. *Noise_distance* is a constant when a constant *Noise_level* is specified. Data set $\{(X,y)\}$ will be fed into the tool, and samples from the set will be used for training.

3.1.1 Initialize Committee with Feedforward Neural Networks

Tensor Flow Keras Sequential model is used for FNN, and the committee is able to initialize with the desired number of FNN models by calling a method.

A list containing multiple positive integers is used to specify the size of the hidden layers. The fist and last element in the list specify the numbers of input and output variables, and the remaining elements are the numbers indicating the number of neurons in the corresponding hidden layer. A list as [2, 50, 40, 30, 3] means that there are 2 input variables in the input layer, 3 outputs in the output layer, and 3 hidden layers with containing 50, 40, 30 neurons respectively.

A list with strings is used to indicate the information of the activation function for each layer in a FNN model. Only the string that is the name of an activation function for Keras sequence models is legal to be the element of the list. For example, ['Relu', 'Sigmoid', 'Tanh', 'Linear'] means that the activation functions from the first layer to the one before the output layer are Relu, Sigmoid, Tanh and Linear functions respectively. The length of an activation-function list is 1 less than that of the corresponding hidden-layer-neuron list.

Based on the introduced list instances, a user can define diverse FNN models to put into the committee, and a special method is designed for simplifying this process. In this method, the number of input and output variables needs to be assigned separately, and the number, n (default in 10), of models and an activation function list with only two elements (default in ['Relu', 'Linear']) can generate a committee with n various FNN models containing 1 to n hidden layers. The number of the neurons (default in 1) for each hidden layer can be a function of i (the numerical order) of the *ith* model in the committee. The activation functions for all the hidden layers will be the first element of the specified activation-function list except for output layers, which use the second element as the activation function.

The parameter to initialize a committee with FNN models are not limited to the hidden layers, number of neurons, and the activation functions introduced here. Other arguments such as Learning Rate, L2 penalty, and Loss Function etc. can also be specified by the user.

3.1.2 Initialize Committee with Regression Trees

Scikit-learn tree regressors are used in the tool, and rules to increase model diversities in the committee are changed according to the specific type of a model. Whether the model is able to become a member of the committee or not depends on its predictions over the training dataset, or the fulfillment of the "interval" fitting policy, which will be introduced in section 3.2.1.

For decision tree regression models, there are two ways to have multiples of them for the committee. One approach is to control the minimum number of samples that are required to split an internal node (the *min_samples_split* parameter), along with setting a least number of models for the committee. A least number is demanded since the "interval" fitting policy (section 3.2.1) might filter out all the models except the fully-grown tree in some situations. The other way is to select all unique sub-sets of two-thirds of the training data set to build the model, along with finding the maximum value of *min_samples_split* fulfilling the "interval" fitting policy.

When using Random Forest Regressor model in this tool, the way of building a committee is to (i) number the training points in observed data set from 1 to n (n is the size of the set) (ii) find out the full permutation of $\{1,\ldots,n\}$; (iii) randomly select k permutations from (ii) and divide every selected one in the middle to have in total $2k$ different sets; (iv) build a Random Forest Regressor model based on the training points corresponding to each set and then put the model into the committee. This method will ensure that there will be $2k$ different models in the committee.

3.1.3 Initialize Committee with Other Models

The advantages of using customized models within the tool are in the adjustment process. Take the neural network model (Multi-layer Perceptron regressor) from Scikit-learn as an example, it is able to be a member of the committee, but the number of neurons in each hidden layer cannot be increased automatically without further adding extra codes or functions, if the model cannot be fitted within the specified iterations or training time.

Beyond the models discussed above, the tool is designed to accept other models to be the member of a committee, if they have "fit" and "prediction" methods, such as the Gaussian Regressor, KNearest Neighbor Regressor, and AdaBoostRegressor from Scikit-learn.

3.2 Training Models from Committee

According to the process of preparing data set for the tool in section 3.1, the gap between y_{noise_free-i} and $y_{noise-i}$ is $Uniform(-1,1) \cdot Noise\_distance$ (Equation 3.1). This gap term means that the error e between y_{noise_free} and y_{noise} fulfills

$$e \sim Uniform(-1,1) \cdot Noise\_level \cdot Max\_distance\_among\_y \tag{3.2}$$

and by using $U(-1,1)$ as the uniform distribution from -1 to 1, its mean and variance are inferred as follows

$$\begin{aligned}
\mu_e &= E[e] = 0 \\
\sigma_e^2 &= E[(e-\mu_e)^2] = E[e^2 - 2e\mu_e + \mu_e^2] = E[e^2] - E[e]^2 \\
&= E[(U(-1,1) \cdot Noise\_level \cdot Max\_distance\_among\_y)^2] \\
&= \left(Var[U(-1,1)] + E[U(-1,1)]^2\right) \cdot (Noise\_level \cdot Max\_distance\_among\_y)^2 \quad (3.3)\\
&= \left(\int_{-1}^{1} \frac{1}{2} x^2 dx + 0^2\right) \cdot (Noise\_level \cdot Max\_distance\_among\_y)^2 \\
&= \frac{1}{3} \cdot (Noise\_level \cdot Max\_distance\_among\_y)^2
\end{aligned}$$

Mean Squared Error (MSE) is commonly used to evaluate how well a model fits a dataset. Based on the variance expression in Equation 3.3, the model is supposed to have perfectly fitted y_{noise_free} data when MSE reaches to $\frac{1}{3} \cdot (Noise\_level \cdot Max\_distance\_among\_y)^2$, and the training process should stop. However, the situation in this project is to make step-wise predictions by just providing a small set of sampling data (6 instances). The feature of only having 6 data points (too less) makes it difficult to further split them into training, test and validation set, and it also imports noises to MSE when evaluating the model.

Denote the given sampling set $T = \{(x_1, y_1), (x_2, y_2), \ldots, (x_n, y_n)\}$ containing n points, and the prediction response of x_i from a model is y_{pred_i}. Then the mean squared prediction error of a model will be $MSE = \frac{1}{n} \sum_{i=1}^{n} (y_{pred\_i} - y_i)^2$. The mean and variance of this MSE is influenced by the size of T, and the probability distribution of the noise within $\{y_i\}$ also poses effects on it. For the problems in real production aimed in this project, the sampling size is small (only 6 for initializing for the experiments in this work) and the noise distribution is unknown. Meanwhile, when setting a MSE threshold into a small value, such as 10^{-5}, there is a risk of overfitting; But if set it in a large value, such as $\frac{1}{n}\sum_{i=1}^{n} y_i$, then there is a risk of model after training being in low prediction accuracy. Therefore the interval policy described below is employed for training the models in committee.

3.2.1 Interval Policy

Interval policy is an adopted strategy for training models in the committee. When fitting a model, a distance of d will be used to determine the boundaries of the prediction values (y_{pred}) over all the training points. After each training epoch of a model, the y_{pred} will be retrieved to compare with the training values (y_{train}). If $|y_{pred} - y_{train}| \leq d$ is satisfied at every training point, then the training process of that model will be stopped, and the model will be considered to be sufficiently trained and ready for predicting the y values of x over the whole search space. Figure 3.1 is an example of this idea, and the predictions at training points 1 to 6 fall between the upper and lower limits (dashed lines).

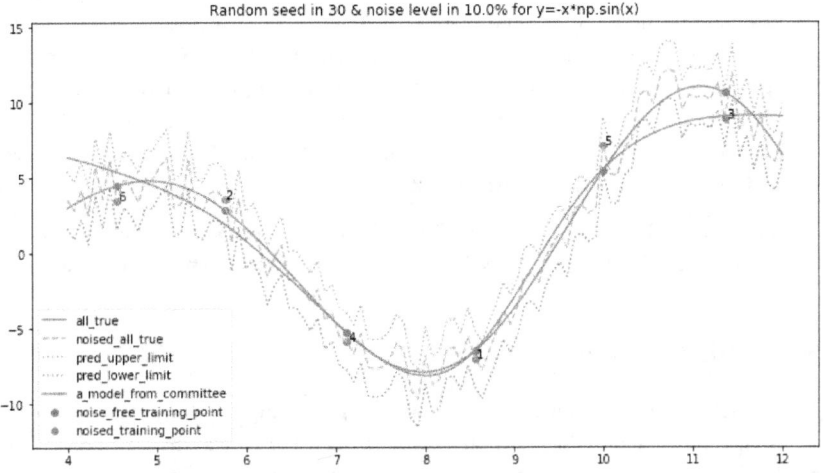

Figure 3.1: Interval training policy introduction

However, this policy is only available to the customized Keras Neural Network Model and the selection of the Scikit-learn Decision Tree Regressor.

3.2.2 Training Models in the Committee

Normally the training process of a FNN model will stop when the number of epochs or the assigned loss criteria (MSE, likelihood, cross entropy, etc.) is met. However, the model may not be well trained within the given training epochs, and increasing the size of training data set makes the situation worse. Setting epoch to a large number as 50000 might be a solution, but it is not efficient especially when a continuous prediction of *x_next* is performed and the network could be too small to fit the data. Thus a mechanism of training time constraint and increasing the number of neurons of the network is adopted and can be activated when training the Neural Network models in the committee.

By the designed mechanism, the training process will stop temporarily for replacing the original model with a new FNN model, which has one neuron more than the previous one, if the training stop criteria is not met within the single time constraint. This process will be repeated until the model is well trained under the selected criteria (MSE or Interval Policy) if a total training time is not set. The total training time constraint is also used to replace the FNN model by a new one with a larger number of neurons increase instead of one by one at certain nodes of the timeline, but it is mainly for deleting a FNN model from the committee if it still cannot fit the data after adding many neurons to the network within the specified total training time scale.

In the above model fitting process, the activation functions and the number of hidden layers of a FNN model will not be changed by the increase of neurons, and the update is only implemented at the number of neurons of each hidden layer. The general idea is to put the extra neuron from the most left to the most right hidden layer and make network grows in a flat way. Suppose that the original hidden layer neuron list is [1, 3, 3, 3, 1], the list will be [1, 4, 3, 3, 1], [1, 4, 4, 3, 1], [1, 4 4, 4, 1], and [1, 5, 4, 4, 1] respectively after adding 1 to 4 neurons to the network.

For the models other than Tensor Flow Keras Neural Network in the committee, the tool has been designed to let the user pass the desired parameters to train the model.

3.3 Predict a x_next

The models from the committee are capable of predicting y values of x in the entire search space after being fitted with the training data. For each x, there will be as many prediction responses as the number of models in the panel, and the criteria to evaluate whether x is a point close to the optimum are based on these predictions.

Depending on the ways of using the uncertainty and variability information of the prediction responses for a x, three different criteria of Expected Improvement are employed to calculate the EI to predict a *x_next* in the toolbox, and they are presented in the first subsection. In case of a singularity occurring when evaluating every x in the search space, a running average of the Expected Improvements can be used as described in the second subsection. To increase the exploration ability of finding the optimum, an ϵ-mechanism is imported into the toolbox and explained in the third subsection.

3.3.1 Different Criteria of Expected Improvement Estimation

Denote that set $U = \{\hat{y}_1(x), \cdots, \hat{y}_n(x)\}$ contains all the prediction responses of x with n being the number of models in the committee, y_{min} is the minimum function value among all the observed data points, and y is the true underlying function value of x. A probability distribution function $p(y|U)$ of y can be obtained by Gaussian Process estimation or Kernel density estimation.

The first criterion for calculating the Expected Improvement is defined in Equation 2.6 in Section 2.2. When using Gaussian density estimation, the mean and variance of $p(y|U)$ are assumed to be the mean and variance of $\{\hat{y}_1(x), \cdots, \hat{y}_n(x)\}$. and the EI of y can be calculated by Equation 2.8. When using Kernel density estimation in normal kernels to have $p(y|U)$, the EI then can be calculated by Equation 2.10, and the rule-of-thumb and cross-validation methods are available for calculating the bandwidth.

The second criterion is defined by specified a τ with $0 < \tau < 1$. After having $p(y|U)$, it is able to find out an unique y_{integ} for the α with $\int_{-\infty}^{y_{integ}} p(y|U) dy = \tau$ and the meaning of y having a probability of τ to be less than y_{integ}. Then the EI of x is defined and calculated by $EI(x) = y_{min} - y_{integ}$.

The third criterion of performing the Expected Improvement estimation is through Interquartile Range (IQR). After obtaining the prediction responses $\{\hat{y}_1(x), \cdots, \hat{y}_n(x)\}$ of a x, the mean and quantiles in such as 25% and 75% can be extracted. By using in-house defined formula $EI(x) = y\_min_{observed} - (y\_mean_{pred} - 2 * (third\_quantile_{pred} - first\_quantile_{pred}))$, an EI for a x can be calculated.

After obtaining the EI for each x in the entire search space by one of the three criteria, comparisons among the EIs of all the candidates will be performed. The x_next leading to the optimal y is considered to be x in maximum EI.

Figure 3.2 shows the first and second criterion of evaluating EI by an example of predicting x_next with four models in the committee. The points of $p1$, $p2$, $p3$, and $p4$ in Figure 3.2(a) were the predicted y values for $x = 7.68$ from *model_1* to *model_4* respectively. Figure 3.2(b) shows an PDF of $p(y|U)$ ($p(y|x = 7.68, p1, p2, p3, p4)$) obtained from Gaussian density estimation; The left graph of it had the EI by the first criterion (Equation 2.8 in Section 2.2), and the EI was the center gravity of the shadowed part by integrating to $y = -6.07$; The right plot in Figure 3.2(b) calculated the EI by second criterion with randomly assigning α to 0.2 (which led to $y_{integ} = -7.23$), and the EI was 1.16 ($= -6.07 - (-7.23) = y_{min} - y_{integ}$).

Figure 3.2(c) illustrates an PDF obtained by Kernel density estimation in normal kernels but with bandwidth by rule-of-thumb (left) and cross validation (right) respectively. In the left figure, the first criterion by Equation 2.10 in Section 2.2 was used to calculate EI, and it was also the center gravity of the shadowed part by integrating to $y = -6.07$; In the right figure used the second criterion to calculate the EI with also randomly

Toolbox Implementation

specifying α to 0.2 (which led to $y_{integ} = -9.27$), and the EI was 3.2 ($= -6.07 - (-9.27) = y_{min} - y_{integ}$).

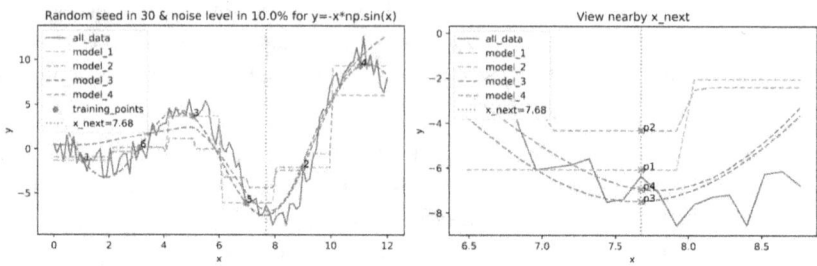

(a) Committee with 4 models to predict x_next

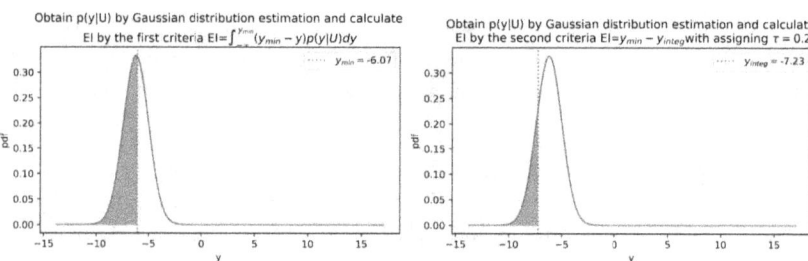

(b) Using Gaussian density estimation to have $p(y|U)$
Using the first criterion (left) and the second criterion (right) to obtain EI

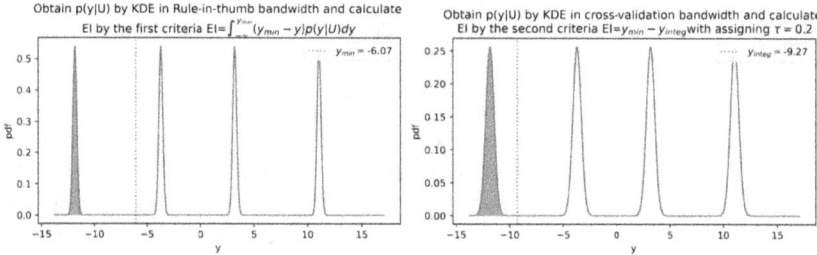

(C) Using Kernel density estimation to have $p(y|U)$
Using the first criterion (left) and the second criterion (right) to obtain EI

Figure 3.2: Different estimation methods of expected improvement

The criteria introduced above for obtaining an EI are flexible, because there are many settings or options for the parameters, such as the bandwidth choice in KDE, the constant coefficient before the subtractions of the quantiles, and the integrating threshold α etc. But the common philosophy here is that choosing *x_next* does not only depend on the mean of the predictions of the y values of a x, the variance of these predictions

Toolbox Implementation

should also be considered. Focus should also be placed on the xs with a relatively lower y_mean_{pred} and/or larger y_var_{pred}.

3.3.2 Running Average of EI

During running tests by the tool, the expected improvement graph often shows narrow peaks. The reason for this might be that the predictions of y values for a set of x within an area changes dramatically, such as the range including points nearby the splitting points of Decision Tree Regression or K-Nearest Neighbor Regression. Except this, in a more general scale, it might be caused by the overfitting of the models in the committee, which leads to the y value predictions in the training points near the same while in other points under huge disagreement.

In order to evaluate the whole search space, a running average of the EIs is able to be performed. A default window size n is assigned to 5, and the size of the new array will be reduced ($(n-1)$ for 1D case and $(w+h-n+1)(n-1)$ for 2D case with w, h being the shape of the 2D array) if the original EI array is not extended. Within the tool, the extension is performed by placing the original array in the center of a proper zero array, and the running average of EI method is only valid for x with 1 or 2 variables (1D or 2D case).

Figure 3.3 is an example of this method for 1D case, and the prediction of x_next according to the maximum EI is shifted to the left after process.

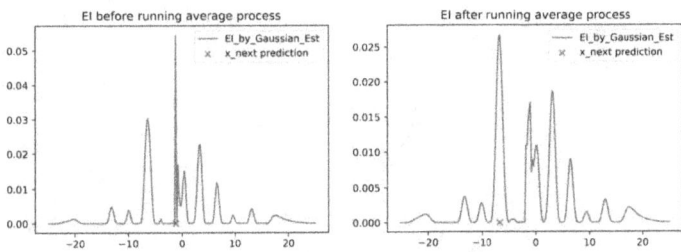

Figure 3.3: Running average process of the Expected Improvements

3.3.3 ϵ-mechanism

An epsilon mechanism (ϵ-mechanism) is introduced for exploration ability, and the general idea is to employ a probability ϵ to change the committee-decided x_next to another x from the search space when the predicted x_next is within a distance threshold (λ, a percentile to avoid the influence of the scale) to any point in the training data set. The purpose of this mechanism is to gain more informative data about the hidden

Toolbox Implementation

function before selecting a *x_next*. The working process of the mechanism is as follows after gaining a *x_next* from the committee.

Step 1:	Generate a random number β from the uniform distribution $[0, 1]$; Continue if $\beta > \epsilon$ (a user-specified probability); Otherwise stop and quit;
Step 2:	Find out the maximum L2 distance d_{max} among all training data points:
Step 3:	Find out the L2 distance vector D between *x_next* and each training point; Calculate $D_p = D/d_{max}$;
Step 4:	Check if there is any element in D_p is smaller than λ (a distance threshold); Continue the process if True, otherwise stop and quit;
Step 5:	Clustering the search space into $n+1$ clusters by KMeans methods; (n is the number of current training points)
Step 6:	Find out the cluster set C containing clusters without any training points, and the cluster C_i from C that has the maximum number of data points;
Step 7:	Find out the point that is closest to the centroid of C_i as the new *x_next*;

According to the study from Dongrui Wu [64], a k-means clustering is employed here because it is able to be applied for the selection of *x_next* to increase the diversity of the training dataset for continuously predicting. Figure 3.4 shows an example of clustering of k-means when the ϵ-mechanism is activated. The defined function related to the clustering part is also able to be used to select the initial training points to be spread out across the search space.

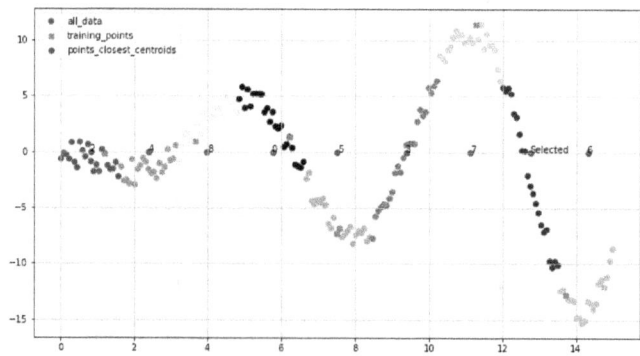

Figure 3.4: K-means clustering for ϵ-mechanism

3.4 Other Methods for Prediction

To prove that the tool actually accelerates the optimization, a random guess method is implemented for comparison. Within this method, the committee model is not used, and the EI, running average of EIs, or ϵ-mechanism are not used. A random selection of x from the search space, except for the current training data points, is used as *x_next*.

One of the main purposes of this thesis project is to evaluate the tool by comparing its performance with GP based Bayesian optimization, thus a method employing a single Gaussian Process regression is implemented in the toolbox. The Scikit learning Gaussian Regressor model is used to predict the mean and variance of y for a x, and then EI can be calculated by Equation 2.7, 2.8 in Section 2.2. Prediction of *x_next* will be the x with maximum EI.

Under the concern of handling high dimension data, a method employed PSO is also developed and included in the toolbox. A training point might be multi-dimensional, and the search space is then expanded exponentially when the dimension increases. If there are n options in each dimension, then for a space with N dimensions, the size of the search space would be in n^N. But the default procedure requires to calculate EI for each point to find the x with maximum EI as *x_next*. The high-dimension problem makes the calculations in this step time consuming or infeasible, and using PSO to find x the optimum EI of a x is one potential solution to this problem.

The objective function in the PSO method has a single x as input and its EI as output. To make this PSO method work for a point in n dimensions in the Python toolbox developed in this project, a numpy.array with shape in $3 \times n$ is designed specially to specify the search space. The first column of the array indicates the type of data. '1' is for continuous data, '2' is for categorized data, and '3' is for encoded data. For continuous data, the second and third columns are the minimum and maximum limits, and any number between the limits will be valid; For categorized data, the second and third columns are the lowest and highest limits, only integer numbers between them will be valid; For encoded (One Hot Encoding) data, the second and third columns are the starting and ending positions of the encoding data; Each encoded group data is valid by having only a '1' and others being in '0', and an encoded group should be in continuous rows. An example in Python code style for search space is as follows, and redundant rows are not reduced in order to simplify the coding of the toolbox. A valid data point x within the defined search space is $numpyp.array([2.2, 0, 1, 0, 3, 8.5, 1, 0])$ in this case.

```
numpy.array([[1,  1.1,  5.1],   # continuous data between 1.1 to 5.1
             [3,  1,    3  ],   # encoded data group 1 from row 1
             [3,  1,    3  ],   # encoded data group 1 with row 2
             [3,  1,    3  ],   # encoded data group 1 ends in row 3
             [2,  0,    5  ],   # categorized data in 0, 1, 2, 3, 4, 5
             [1, -10,  20  ],   # continuous data between -10 to 20
             [3,  6,    7  ],   # encoded data group 2 from row 6
             [3,  6,    7  ],   # encoded data group 2 ends in row 7
             ])
```

3.5 Results Comparison and Function Generator

Candidate points of a function defining candidate experiments used are sampled from a predefined search space, and there are chances that only the neighboring points of the optimum are selected. Beyond this, different noise levels will be used to generate testing data sets from the same function. Therefore, the way of accepting a *x_next* as sufficiently good to be considered as the optimum should relate to the noise level. Figure 3.5 is an example from this principle.

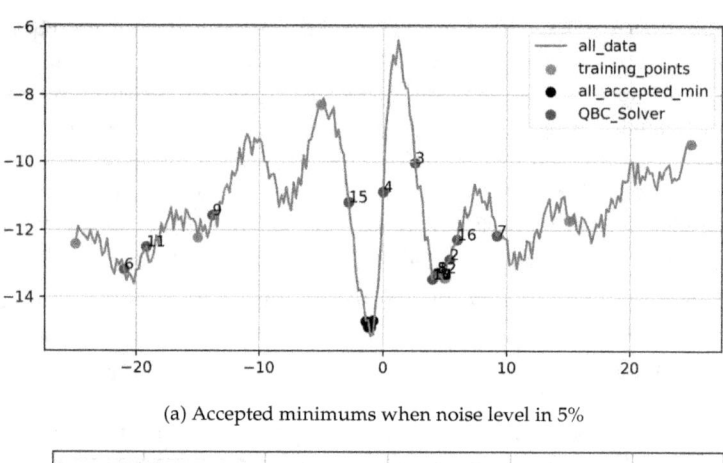

(a) Accepted minimums when noise level in 5%

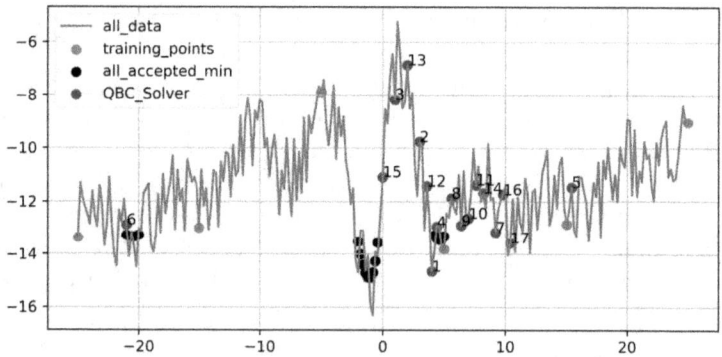

(b) Accepted minimums when noise level in 20%

Figure 3.5: Accepted minima according to noise level

Figure 3.5 shows a continuous 17 predictions of *x_next* by QBC with committee built by FNNs for two sets of data from one function but with noise level 5% and 20% respectively, and the points marked in black are considered as accepted minima solutions. As introduced in section 3.1, when a noise level in percentage is assigned to generate testing data, a *Noise_distance* will be calculated and a y_{min} among all sampled y will be extracted. Once the y value of a predicted *x_next* is less or equal than $y_{min} -$ *Noise_distance*, the corresponding *x_next* will be considered as an accepted minimum. Thus, Figure 3.5(b) has a wider range of accepted minimum than Figure 3.5(a).

To make it convenient for testing in different functions with x in 1D or 2D, a function generator [65] is implemented in the solver. By assigning the lower and upper limit of the definition domain and the dimension information of x, a random function will be returned. And if a same random seed is also specified every time, then the returned function will be the same when run the code each time, otherwise, the returned function might be different.

4 Tests and Results

When comparing the performance of AL being done by using GP and by using QBC, one method is considered better if it takes less steps to get to the optimum function value. One way of finding out the number of needed steps in the experiment is to count the consumed steps until the real minimum is found. But in this way the running time of each method is hard to control since the number of the required steps is unknown. Thus the other strategy is to run all methods for a given number of steps and then to check in which step the method predicts an *x_next* within the range of acceptance. Examples to illustrate the chosen strategy and the toolbox working process are presented in the first section, and comparison experiments are presented in the sections after.

Functions used for those examples and experiment are all from the Appendix A, which contains 17 functions with x in 1D (section A.1) and 13 functions with x in 2D (section A.2). Except the ones referenced from the Internet [66, 67], others were generated by the function generator coded inside the toolbox by specifying a random seed and a domain range. Detailed information for functions with x in 1D and 2D including function expressions, plots and definition domains can be found from Figure A.1 and Figure A.2 in the appendix. Two functions with x in 3D used for comparison experiment are listed as below, since they cannot be presented in a graph as those with x in 1D and 2D, and all of them are defined with the domain in $x_1, x_2, x_3 \in [-4, -4]$.

$$f(x_1, x_2, x_3) = 0.5 \log_e \left((x_1+1)^2 + (x_2-2)^2 + (x_3-1)^2 + 0.25 \right) \tag{3D\_1}$$

$$f(x_1, x_2, x_3) = 0.05 \left[(x_1^4 - 16x_1^2 + 5x_1) + (x_2^4 - 16x_2^2 + 5x_2) + (x_3^4 - 16x_1^2 + 5x_3) \right] \tag{3D\_2}$$

4.1 Test Examples

4.1.1 1D Example

Function below [18] (Appendix 1D function 17) with x in $[0, 1.01]$ and a noise level 5% was used to generate data, and its optimum is located at around $x = 0.76$.

$$f(x) = (6x - 2)^2 \sin(12x - 4)$$

Tests and Results

This example was carried out under a continuous 5 predictions of *x_next* with 6 initial training points for finding an acceptable minimum function value by QBC (with committee built by 3 FNN models), GP and the random guess method separately. Within the QBC approach, normal distribution along with the first criterion presented in Section 3.3.1 was used for the calculation of EI. The ϵ-mechanism was activated, but the running average of EI method was not.

Figure 4.1 contains information for the 5th predictions of *x_next* by QBC, GP and the random guess method respectively. From Figure 4.1a, QBC predicted the optimum to be located at $x = 0.77$, GP method had it at the second step with $x = 0.76$ (point 8*th* in Figure 4.1b), and the random guess method did not find the optimum within its 5 steps (Figure 4.1c).

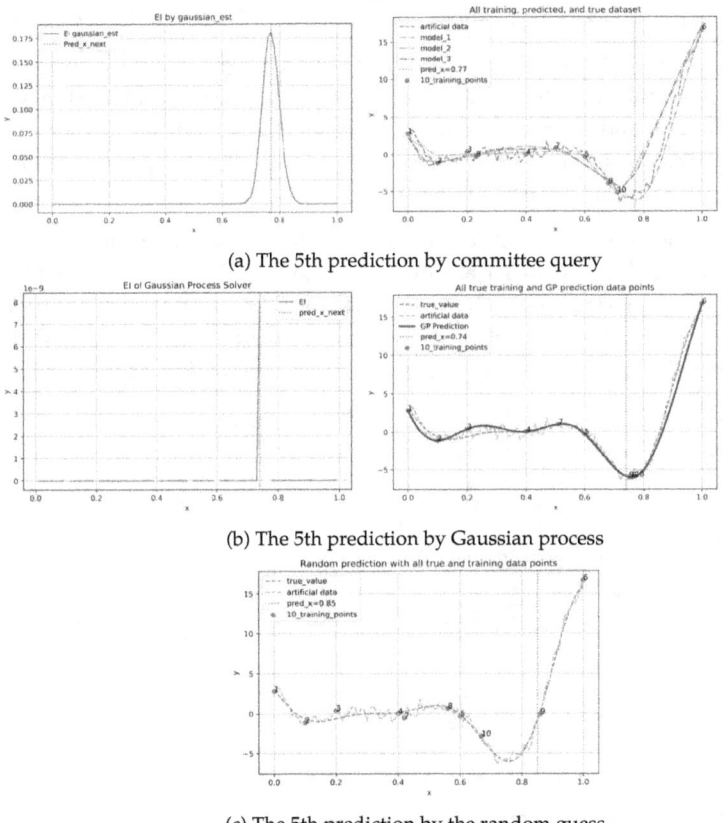

(a) The 5th prediction by committee query

(b) The 5th prediction by Gaussian process

(c) The 5th prediction by the random guess

Figure 4.1: A case of 1D function with the 5th prediction of *x_next*

Tests and Results

Thus in this example, GP outperformed QBC method. The predicting processes for the previous 4 steps of these 3 methods are attached in the appendix section B.1 Figure set B.2.

4.1.2 2D Example

For x in 2D, the function below [68] (Appendix 2D function 13) with $x_1, x_2 \in [0, -5]$ and a noise level 5% was used to create the artificial data for this example,

$$f(x_1, x_2) = -0.7e^{\frac{(x_1-1)^2 + (x_2-1)^2}{-0.18}} - 0.75e^{\frac{(x_1-1)^2 + (x_2-3)^2}{-0.32}}$$
$$- e^{\frac{(x_1-3)^2 + (x_2-1)^2}{-2}} - 1.2e^{\frac{(x_1-3)^2 + (x_2-4)^2}{-0.32}} - e^{\frac{(x_1-5)^2 + (x_2-2)^2}{-0.72}}$$

and the true unknown global minimum of this function is at (3, 4) in the defined domain.

This example was set to make 15 predictions of *x_next* by QBC, GP and the random guess method separately. Within this test, the committee of QBC was based on 20 random forest tree models, and normal distribution along with the first criterion presented in Section 3.3.1 were used to for the calculation of EI. The ϵ-mechanism was also activated while the running average on the EI was not.

Figure set 4.2 shows the eighth prediction by QBC (Figure 4.2b), GP (Figure 4.2c) and the random guess (Figure 4.2a). An accepted minimum was first found by the QBC at the eighth prediction. Figure set B.3 in appendix section B.2 contains the previous seven predictions and the final statistics of predicted *x_next* by different methods (Figure B.3). In this case QBC with committee consisting of RT models outperformed the other two methods.

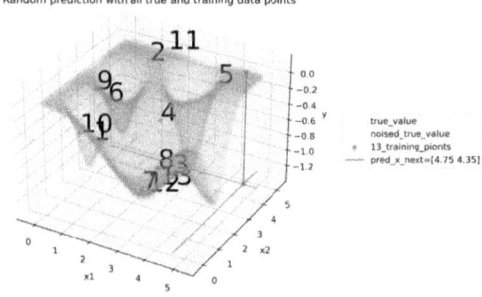

(a) The 8th prediction by the random guess

Figure 4.2: A case of 2D function with the 8th prediction of *x_next*

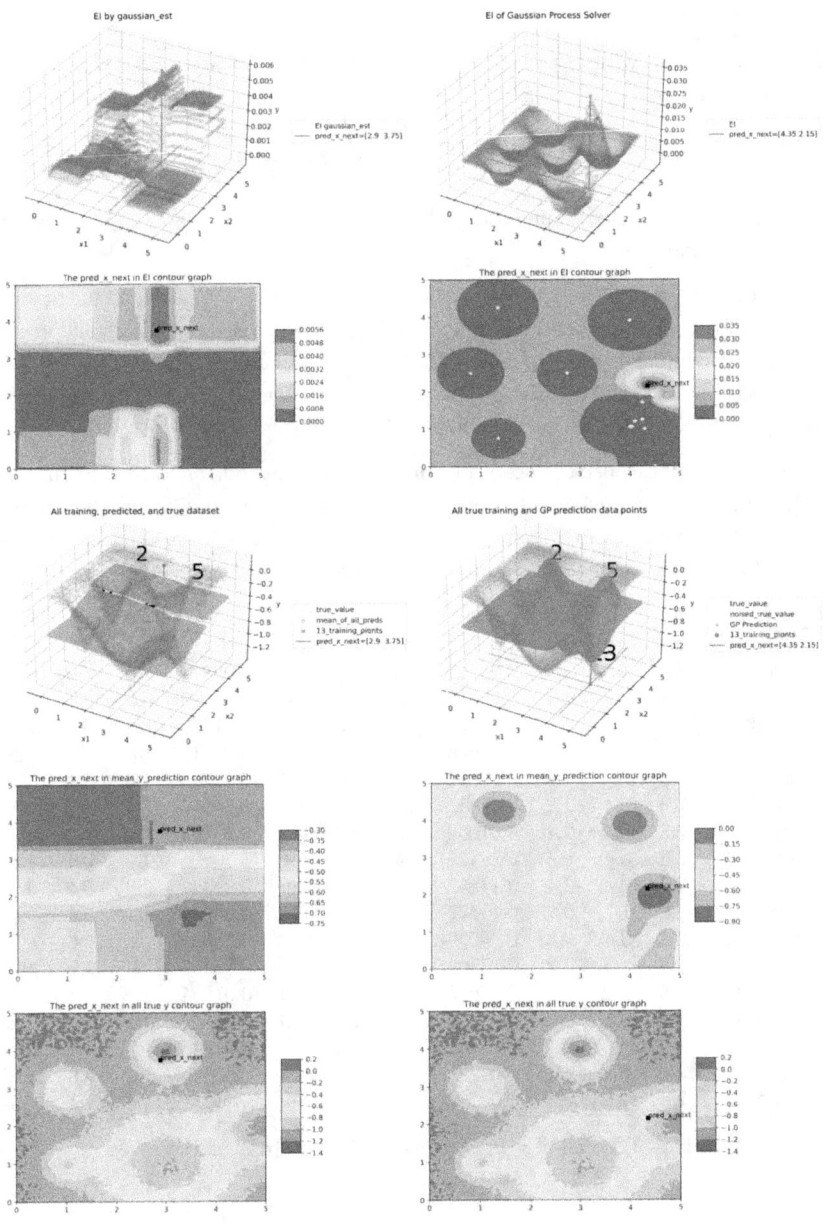

(b) The 8th prediction by committee query   (c) The 8th prediction by Gaussian process

Figure 4.2: A case of 2D function with the 8th prediction of x_next

4.1.3 3D Example

The function below with $x_1, x_2, x_3 \in [-4, -4]$ and noise level 7% was used to gain samples in 3 dimensions,

$$f(x_1, x_2, x_3) = 0.5 \log_e \left((x_1 - 1.2)^2 + (x_2 + 2.3)^2 + (x_3 - 0.5)^2 + 0.25 \right)$$

and the true desired global minimum of this function is located at $(-1.2, 2.3, 0.5)$ within the given domain.

The test was performed to make 17 predictions of *x_next* by QBC, GP and the random guess method separately, and the committee of QBC was based on 9 Gaussian process models with different parameters, and KDE with the first criterion presented in Section 3.3.1 was used for the EI calculation. The ϵ-mechanism was activated while the running average of EI was not available for *x* higher than 2 dimensions.

Table 4.1 contains detailed prediction of *x_next* for each method. On these 17 predictions, GP reached to an acceptable minimum at the 8th evaluation, while QBC and the random guess did not have any prediction as an acceptable minimum. Thus, Gaussian Process outperformed QBC with the configurations used here.

Prediction	QBC				GP				Random Guess		
	x_1	x_2	x_3	EI	x_1	x_2	x_3	EI	x_1	x_2	x_3
Pred_1	3.4	-0.8	2	0.00912	3.4	-1	2.2	0.03811	3.6	-0.4	-3.4
Pred_2	2.8	0.2	1.4	0.00113	4	-4	4	0.18990	-1.2	-1.6	-0.4
Pred_3	2.4	0.2	1.4	0.01472	4	-0.6	2.8	0.01826	0.4	0.4	2.6
Pred_4	2.8	0.6	1.2	0.00038	3.2	-1.2	1.8	0.03013	0	2	2.6
Pred_5	2.8	0	1.4	0.00010	3	-1.6	1.2	0.09265	1.8	-2.4	-0.4
Pred_6	2.8	0.4	1.8	0.02741	3	-2.8	-0.2	0.30652	3.4	-0.2	-2
Pred_7	2.8	0.4	1.4	0.01008	2.6	-2.2	0.4	0.12798	3.4	1.4	-3.8
Pred_8	2.8	0.4	0.6	0.29462	**1.4**	**-2.4**	**0.4**	0.33136	1.4	0.4	1.8
Pred_9	2.8	0	2.4	0.14887	0.6	-2.8	0.6	0.32344	0.8	-3.2	3.2
Pred_10	2.6	1.2	0.8	0.13372	1.2	-2	0.2	0.08017	-0.6	3.4	2.8
Pred_11	2.8	0.6	0.8	0.06679	1.4	-2.2	1	0.05066	-2	0.6	-3.8
Pred_12	2.8	1.6	1.2	0.15394	1.4	-2.8	0	0.05053	2	1.6	-0.8
Pred_13	2.8	-0.2	0.4	0.12667	1.2	-2.4	0.6	0.01554	-2.8	-3.4	-2.8
Pred_14	2.8	0.2	0.8	0.06011	1.4	-2.8	0.8	0.01069	2.4	-0.2	-1.2
Pred_15	2.8	0	-0.2	0.16443	1	-2.2	0.6	0.01848	4	-1.6	0.6
Pred_16	3	0	2	0.04799	1.2	-2.4	0.4	0.00897	4	3.8	-2.6
Pred_17	2.8	-0.2	0.6	0.00507	1.8	4	-4	0.01299	0.4	-0.6	-3.2

Table 4.1: Detail of *x_next* for 17 predictions from each method

4.2 Comparing GP with QBC in FNN Committee

Table 4.2 containes the information and results of the comparison between GP and QBC with committee built by FNN models. Here the number of the FNN models in the committee and the initial parameters of the models were all different from those used for the presented 1D example in Section 4.1.1. In this experiment, each method had ran 17 evaluations of *x_next* for finding an acceptable minimum of a function.

No	Function	Noise Level in 0.05					Noise Level in 0.2				
		Q	G	R	QvsG	QvsR	Q	G	R	QvsG	QvsR
1	1D_1	2	2	5	Same	QBC	1	1	5	Same	QBC
2	1D_2	5	2	N	GP	QBC	4	1	7	GP	QBC
3	1D_3	1	6	2	QBC	QBC	2	1	1	GP	Rand
4	1D_4	11	6	3	GP	Rand	7	14	3	QBC	Rand
5	1D_5	1	1	1	Same	Same	1	1	1	Same	Same
6	1D_6	1	1	7	Same	QBC	1	3	6	QBC	QBC
7	1D_7	6	4	3	GP	Rand	1	1	N	Same	QBC
8	1D_8	1	1	8	Same	QBC	1	1	2	Same	QBC
9	1D_9	3	15	N	QBC	QBC	4	9	9	QBC	QBC
10	1D_10	5	6	15	QBC	QBC	9	7	8	GP	Rand
11	1D_11	4	1	2	GP	Rand	6	1	11	GP	QBC
12	1D_12	14	10	N	GP	QBC	N	3	N	GP	NK
13	1D_13	4	8	17	QBC	QBC	4	1	2	GP	Rand
14	1D_14	5	13	N	QBC	QBC	N	3	16	GP	Rand
15	1D_15	16	N	8	QBC	Rand	16	6	11	GP	Rand
16	1D_16	4	N	N	QBC	QBC	2	16	12	QBC	QBC
17	2D_1	N	N	N	NK	NK	N	6	N	GP	NK
18	2D_2	N	N	N	NK	NK	N	N	N	NK	NK
19	2D_3	2	1	1	GP	Rand	4	2	7	GP	QBC
20	2D_4	2	N	1	QBC	Rand	5	N	1	QBC	Rand
21	2D_5	2	1	1	GP	Rand	4	1	1	GP	Rand
22	2D_6	5	N	N	QBC	QBC	5	N	N	QBC	QBC
23	2D_7	N	N	N	NK	NK	6	2	3	GP	Rand
24	2D_8	N	14	N	GP	NK	8	10	N	QBC	QBC
25	2D_9	N	N	N	NK	NK	12	11	N	GP	QBC
26	2D_10	N	N	N	NK	NK	2	N	N	QBC	QBC
27	2D_11	N	N	N	NK	NK	N	1	15	GP	Rand
28	2D_12	N	N	N	NK	NK	N	4	N	GP	NK
29	3D_1	14	8	N	GP	QBC	N	7	N	GP	NK
30	3D_2	N	N	N	NK	NK	N	1	13	GP	Rand

Table 4.2: Compare GP with QBC in FNN committee

QBC vs GP	Q	GP	Same	NK	QBC vs Rand	Q	Rand	Same	NK
NL in 0.05	9	9	4	8	NL in 0.05	13	7	1	9
NL in 0.20	8	17	4	1	NL in 0.20	13	11	1	5
Sum	17	26	8	9	Sum	26	18	2	14

Table 4.3: Summary of Table 4.2

The notations in the table are explained as following, and they are also used in other tables of the comparison experiment. The "Function" column shows tests in different functions, and "1D_3" means the third 1D function from the function pool in appendix, while "3D_1" and "3D_2" are referred to Function 3D_1 and 3D_2 at the beginning of this chapter. The columns with capital letter "Q", "G", and "R" contains in which step the QBC, GP and the random guess approach respectively find an acceptable minimum; Column filled with "N" means that the correspond method had not found an acceptable minimum within the specified running evaluations of x_next. Column "QvsG" and "QvsR" stand the comparison between QBC and GP method for doing Active Learning optimization, and comparison between QBC and the random guess method respectively. The contents in those columns show which method outperforms; "NK" means Not Known when both methods have not found an acceptable minimum; and "Same" means two methods use same number of evaluations to reach to an acceptable minimum.

Line number 14 is explained here as an example. This test was performed over the 14th 1D function from the appended function pool. When generating testing data by noise level 0.05 and running 17 evaluations, QBC found an acceptable minimum at the 5th prediction, GP found one at the 13th prediction, and the random guess did not found any acceptable minimum. Thus when compare QBC with GP, QBC outperformed, and when compare QBC with the random guess, QBC still outperformed. While when generating testing data with noise level in 0.2 and running 17 evaluations, QBC did not find any acceptable minimum, GP found one at the 3rd prediction, and the random guess found one at the 16th prediction. Thus when compare QBC with GP, GP outperformed, and when compare QBC with the random guess method, the random guess outperformed.

The shared settings for all the tests in this and the other comparison experiments were that there were 6 initial training points picked from the generated artificial data to start the evaluation, and the running average of EI (only avaible for x in 1D and 2D cases) and ϵ-mechanism were all activated. The mentioned QBC in each experiment was a QBC with the specific settings for the experiment, and the settings were different. Meanwhile, the method employed for estimating the probability distribution of the prediction responses for a x was Gaussian distribution estimation in default if it was not specified, and the first criterion presented in Section 3.3.1 was used for EI calculation.

There were 7 FNN models in the committee of QBC, and they had from 1 to 5 hidden layers. The initial numbers of neurons for each hidden layer were different by choosing from 20, 30, and 50. The activation functions used in this experiment were Tanh, Sigmoid and Linear. During the training process, the number of neurons were increased if it cannot fulfill the interval policy. If the model cannot fit the training data for a long time, then it would be removed from the committee. This led to sometimes there was only two or one, or even none committee member left. In those cases, the process was then restarted to continue with changing the training policy to MSE with epochs for training into 50000.

The results statistic of this comparison shows in Table 4.3. For those 30 functions and 60 tests (two different noise levels were used for each function to generate data for a test), QBC proved its validity through its better performance (8 times more to reach an acceptable minimum earlier) than using the random guess method, and GP was the better than QBC by outperforming 26 times, which were mainly from the tests with noise level in 0.2. GP and QBC ended in a tie when noise level in 0.05, and the Not Known case of the comparison result reduced sharply from 8 to 1 when the noise level was increased.

4.3 Compare GP with QBC in RT Committee

As presented in section 3.1.2 in previous chapter, different tree methods for building the committee had been designed, and they were all used to construct the committee in this experiment. Table 4.4 contains the information and results of the comparison between GP and QBC with committee built on RT (including Random Forest) models, and Table 4.5 shows a brief summary of the results.

No	Function	Noise Level in 0.05					Noise Level in 0.2				
		Q	G	R	QvsG	QvsR	Q	G	R	QvsG	QvsR
1	1D_1	1	2	9	QBC	QBC	1	1	5	Same	QBC
2	1D_2	3	2	8	GP	QBC	3	1	1	GP	Rand
3	1D_3	2	6	3	QBC	QBC	1	1	3	Same	QBC
4	1D_4	3	4	N	QBC	QBC	9	N	N	QBC	QBC
5	1D_5	1	1	1	Same	Same	1	1	1	Same	Same
6	1D_6	3	1	8	GP	QBC	6	3	1	GP	Rand
7	1D_7	2	4	N	QBC	QBC	2	1	9	GP	QBC
8	1D_8	6	1	5	GP	Rand	2	1	1	GP	Rand
9	1D_9	10	N	N	QBC	QBC	N	N	N	NK	NK
10	1D_10	8	6	1	GP	Rand	10	7	N	GP	QBC
11	1D_11	2	1	8	GP	QBC	1	1	6	Same	QBC
12	1D_12	N	10	N	GP	NK	N	3	9	GP	Rand
13	1D_13	5	8	N	QBC	QBC	N	1	5	GP	Rand
14	1D_14	1	N	1	QBC	Same	1	3	2	QBC	QBC
15	1D_15	N	N	N	NK	NK	3	6	N	QBC	QBC
16	1D_16	N	N	N	NK	NK	N	N	1	NK	Rand
17	2D_1	N	N	N	NK	NK	N	6	N	GP	NK
18	2D_2	N	N	N	NK	NK	N	N	N	NK	NK
19	2D_3	3	1	2	GP	Rand	1	2	1	QBC	Same
20	2D_4	4	N	8	QBC	QBC	1	N	1	QBC	Same
21	2D_5	2	1	2	GP	Same	1	1	1	Same	Same
22	2D_6	3	N	N	QBC	QBC	1	N	N	QBC	QBC
23	2D_7	N	N	N	NK	NK	2	2	N	Same	QBC
24	2D_8	N	N	N	NK	NK	N	10	N	GP	NK
25	2D_9	N	N	N	NK	NK	5	11	9	QBC	QBC
26	2D_10	N	N	N	NK	NK	N	N	N	NK	NK
27	2D_11	N	N	N	NK	NK	2	1	N	GP	QBC
28	2D_12	N	N	N	NK	NK	N	4	N	GP	NK
29	3D_1	N	8	N	GP	NK	N	7	N	GP	NK
30	3D_2	N	N	N	NK	NK	N	1	N	GP	NK

Table 4.4: Compare GP with QBC in GP committee

QBC vs GP	Q	GP	Same	NK	QBC vs Rand	Q	Rand	Same	NK
NL in 0.05	9	9	1	11	NL in 0.05	11	3	3	13
NL in 0.20	7	13	6	4	NL in 0.20	12	6	4	8
Sum	16	22	7	15	Sum	23	9	7	21

Table 4.5: Summary of table 4.4

One of the method to build a model for the committee was to select two thirds of the training data to construct a RT, and that would result in many selections when the base was large. For example there would be $\binom{18}{12} = 18564$ unique subsets when select 12 ($= 18 \times \frac{2}{3}$) points from a total 18 different training data point. The size of the training data set would increase one after making each prediction/evaluation of x_next. When building and training the models with conducting many predictions, it might be risky to have too many models in the committee (computation expensive or infeasible). Thus, the number of evaluations of x_next in this experiment was limited to 12 since it was initialized with 6 training data points, and the numbers of committee members in QBC for each evaluation were different from 25 to 18000 or even more.

The rule of using two-thirds of the training data to build a model is only applied for building conventional Regression Tree model (this portion value is from user experience), because when using the whole but a small number (6 for initializing) of the data points to build RT models, they are easy to be overfitting and similar. Using the subsets will change the situation and improve the diversities of the committee.

For all 60 tests over the 30 functions, QBC outperformed the random guess method regarding both on the number and the used iterations of finding an acceptable optimum, but GP was the best among these three methods when just considering using less predictions to to reach an acceptable (close to global) optimum minimum. QBC and GP also ended in a tie for tests with noise level 5%. The Not Known case of the comparison result reduced sharply from 11 to 4 when the noise level was increased.

4.4 Compare GP with QBC in GP Committee by Using Normal Distribution to Calculate EI

Table 4.6 contains the information and results of the comparison between GP and QBC with committee built on 9 different GP models, and Table 4.7 is a simple statistics of the results. The number of predictions of x_next was set into 17.

No	Function	Noise Level in 0.05					Noise Level in 0.2				
		Q	G	R	QvsG	QvsR	Q	G	R	QvsG	QvsR
1	1D_1	2	2	N	Same	QBC	1	1	14	Same	QBC
2	1D_2	1	2	N	QBC	QBC	2	1	3	GP	QBC

Table 4.6: Compare GP with QBC in GP committee continue...

No	Function	Noise Level in 0.05					Noise Level in 0.2				
		Q	G	R	QvsG	QvsR	Q	G	R	QvsG	QvsR
3	1D_3	1	6	N	QBC	QBC	1	1	1	Same	Same
4	1D_4	3	4	5	QBC	QBC	6	N	8	QBC	QBC
5	1D_5	1	1	2	Same	QBC	1	1	2	Same	QBC
6	1D_6	1	1	12	Same	QBC	2	3	1	QBC	Rand
7	1D_7	4	4	N	Same	QBC	1	1	16	Same	QBC
8	1D_8	1	1	3	Same	QBC	1	1	1	Same	Same
9	1D_9	15	15	N	Same	QBC	14	9	N	GP	QBC
10	1D_10	15	6	N	GP	QBC	N	7	4	GP	Rand
11	1D_11	1	1	N	Same	QBC	4	1	13	GP	QBC
12	1D_12	6	10	12	QBC	QBC	15	3	16	GP	QBC
13	1D_13	4	8	8	QBC	QBC	2	1	14	GP	QBC
14	1D_14	4	13	N	QBC	QBC	N	3	N	GP	NK
15	1D_15	N	N	N	NK	NK	4	6	N	QBC	QBC
16	1D_16	15	17	N	QBC	QBC	13	16	N	QBC	QBC
17	2D_1	17	N	N	QBC	QBC	N	6	N	GP	NK
18	2D_2	N	N	N	NK	NK	N	N	N	NK	NK
19	2D_3	1	1	N	Same	QBC	1	2	12	QBC	QBC
20	2D_4	N	N	9	NK	Rand	7	N	1	QBC	Rand
21	2D_5	2	1	11	GP	QBC	3	1	2	GP	Rand
22	2D_6	4	N	N	QBC	QBC	2	N	N	QBC	QBC
23	2D_7	N	N	N	NK	NK	1	2	8	QBC	QBC
24	2D_8	N	14	N	GP	NK	4	10	N	QBC	QBC
25	2D_9	11	N	N	QBC	QBC	2	9	N	QBC	QBC
26	2D_10	N	N	N	NK	NK	N	7	14	GP	Rand
27	2D_11	3	N	N	QBC	QBC	1	1	6	Same	QBC
28	2D_12	10	N	N	QBC	QBC	N	4	N	GP	NK
29	3D_1	4	8	N	QBC	QBC	12	7	N	GP	QBC
30	3D_2	N	N	N	NK	NK	1	1	11	Same	QBC

Table 4.6: Compare GP with QBC in GP committee

QBC vs GP	Q	GP	Same	NK	QBC vs Rand	Q	Rand	Same	NK
NL in 0.05	13	3	8	6	NL in 0.05	23	1	0	6
NL in 0.20	10	12	7	1	NL in 0.20	19	5	2	4
Sum	23	15	15	7	Sum	42	6	2	10

Table 4.7: Summary of Table 4.6

Based on the summary on the right part of Table 4.7, most of the time QBC was able to found the optimum or found the optimum earlier than the random guess method. Thus QBC was valid for accelerating the optimizing process.

Tests and Results   45

From the results in the left part of Table 4.7, when came to count the used predictions for gaining an acceptable minimum, QBC with ensembles of GP models performed better than a single GP model, because QBC had 23 times earlier in total than GP to gain an acceptable minimum out of the 60 tests while GP just had 15 times faster than QBC. When considered the noise level for this experiment, QBC was almost dominant the single GP method when noise level was 0.05, since QBC had 13 times earlier gaining an acceptable minimum while GP just had 3 times faster than QBC; Although QBC had 10 times earlier than the single GP method, it still lost 2 times to the single GP when noise level was 0.2. The Not Known case of the comparison result reduced sharply from 6 to 1 when the noise level was increased.

4.5 Compare GP with QBC in GP Committee by Using KDE to Calculate EI

Table 4.8 contains the information and results of the comparison between GP and QBC with committee built on Gaussian Process models, but this comparison experiment differed from the previous one by using KDE within QBC to calculate EI for each candidate point. Table 4.9 is a simple statistics of the results. The number of predictions of x_next was also set into 17.

No	Function	Noise Level in 0.05					Noise Level in 0.2				
		Q	G	R	QvsG	QvsR	Q	G	R	QvsG	QvsR
1	1D_1	2	2	N	Same	QBC	1	1	16	Same	QBC
2	1D_2	1	2	N	QBC	QBC	2	1	16	GP	QBC
3	1D_3	1	6	N	QBC	QBC	1	1	1	Same	Same
4	1D_4	3	4	5	QBC	QBC	6	N	8	QBC	QBC
5	1D_5	1	1	2	Same	QBC	1	1	4	Same	QBC
6	1D_6	1	1	12	Same	QBC	3	3	9	Same	QBC
7	1D_7	3	4	N	QBC	QBC	1	1	15	Same	QBC
8	1D_8	1	1	4	Same	QBC	1	1	1	Same	Same
9	1D_9	16	15	N	GP	QBC	N	9	16	GP	Rand
10	1D_10	10	6	N	GP	QBC	9	7	2	GP	Rand
11	1D_11	1	1	N	Same	QBC	1	1	8	Same	QBC
12	1D_12	N	10	N	GP	NK	N	3	8	GP	Rand
13	1D_13	14	8	N	GP	QBC	3	1	N	GP	QBC
14	1D_14	N	13	N	GP	NK	N	3	N	GP	NK
15	1D_15	N	N	N	NK	NK	6	6	N	Same	QBC
16	1D_16	N	N	N	NK	NK	13	16	N	QBC	QBC
17	2D_1	N	N	N	NK	NK	N	6	N	GP	NK
18	2D_2	17	N	N	QBC	QBC	N	N	N	NK	NK

Table 4.8: Compare GP with QBC committeed by GP models when using KDE for EI

No	Function	Noise Level in 0.05					Noise Level in 0.2				
		Q	G	R	QvsG	QvsR	Q	G	R	QvsG	QvsR
19	2D_3	1	1	N	Same	QBC	1	2	12	QBC	QBC
20	2D_4	12	N	3	QBC	Rand	4	N	1	QBC	Rand
21	2D_5	1	1	10	Same	QBC	1	1	3	Same	QBC
22	2D_6	3	N	N	QBC	QBC	3	N	N	QBC	QBC
23	2D_7	N	N	N	NK	NK	1	2	4	QBC	QBC
24	2D_8	N	14	N	GP	NK	N	10	N	GP	NK
25	2D_9	N	N	N	NK	NK	2	9	N	QBC	QBC
26	2D_10	N	N	N	NK	NK	N	N	14	NK	Rand
27	2D_11	3	N	N	QBC	QBC	1	1	8	Same	QBC
28	2D_12	N	N	N	NK	NK	N	4	N	GP	NK
29	3D_1	4	8	N	QBC	QBC	6	7	N	QBC	QBC
30	3D_2	N	N	N	NK	NK	N	1	11	GP	Rand

Table 4.8: Compare GP with QBC committeed by GP models when using KDE for EI

QBC vs GP	Q	GP	Same	NK	QBC vs Rand	Q	Rand	Same	NK
NL in 0.05	9	6	7	8	NL in 0.05	18	1	0	11
NL in 0.20	8	10	10	2	NL in 0.20	17	6	2	5
Sum	17	16	17	10	Sum	35	7	2	16

Table 4.9: Summary of Table 4.8

QBC in the settings used for this experiment was also valid since it had 35 times earlier than the random guess method to reach an acceptable minimum. When comparing GP and the QBC, QBC slightly outperformed GP since within the 60 tests it had 17 times earlier reaching an optimum while GP had 16 times earlier than QBC. When considering the noise level used for the tests, QBC only outperformed 3 times when noise level in 0.05, which reduced dramatically compared the results of using normal distribution to calculate EIs. The Not Known case of the comparison result reduced sharply from 8 to 2 when the noise level was increased to 0.2.

4.6 Application in Industrial Simulation Problem

An automation manufacturing production line usually assembles many machines with abilities of running in different settings, such as the capacity of a buffer and the running speed of a shuttle line. Targets as increasing production rate, reducing production cost or lowering down inventory can be turned into problems of finding out a proper set of settings for all machines in the system, that is gaining a vector x to have the optimum $f(x)$ of a hidden and possibly computation-expensive function f. Often discrete-event simulation technology is employed for simulating the scenarios, and this kind of problems are solved by the optimization algorithms.

Problem as such also matches the intention of this project, thus the selected industrial problem was to find the optimum of key performance indicators including Throughput, Lead Time (LT) and Work In Process (WIP) of a production system from hidden/unknown functions $f_1, f_2, and f_3$ defined as follows

$$Throughput = f_1(availability\ set, process\_time\ set, buffer\_size\ set) \quad (4.2)$$
$$WIP = f_2(availability\ set, process\_time\ set, buffer\_size\ set) \quad (4.3)$$
$$LT = f_3(availability\ set, process\_time\ set, buffer\_size\ set) \quad (4.4)$$

The (discrete-event) simulation of the production system was performed by FACTS Analyzer [69], and the optimization of the problems was conducted by QBC and FACTS Analyzer at the same time for a simple comparison.

FACTS Analyzer is an Internet-based Discrete-Event-Simulation and Simulation-Based-Optimization software system that contains many tools for optimal decision making. Various components including optimization algorithms, ANN based meta models, stochastic simulation systems and a SQL database management system are integrated inside it and available to users. With the abilities of automatically generating models based on optimization parameters, and gaining Pareto-optimal solutions, FACTS Analyzer enables and provides simulation for supporting the design, analysis and improvement of production systems within a multi-objective context. [69, 70]

While FACTS Analyzer is able to performs optimization in an iterative format by using different optimization engines, such as Nondominated Sorting Genetic Algorithm (NSGA-II), Differential Evolution, and Covariance Matrix Adaptation with evolution strategy etc. NSGA-II [71] as a multi-objective evolutionary algorithms was used for the tests here with setting the number of evaluation to 1500 and the population size to 50. The algorithm along with its working process for the simulation optimization in FACTS Analyze are introduced below.

After defining a simulation model and setting the related parameters for the simulation, it is ready for configuring the search space, constraints, objectives and other parameters of the optimization. After launching the process with the configurations, the simulation and optimization engine works as (1) simulating each candidate in a parent population (randomly generated when initializing) for gaining the fitness; (2) obtaining offspring by crossover and mutation after selection; (3) gaining the fitness of each offspring by simulation evaluation; (4) perform fast elitist nondominated sorting; (5) grouping an updated parent population by selecting the solutions on or close to rank 1 (Pareto Front) and rejecting candidates; (6) repeat the steps from (1) to (5) until meeting the stop criteria.

Since QBC with committee build by GP models and using normal distribution estimation for calculating EI performed best in the comparison experiments, QBC with the same setup (butnthe parameters for GP models in the committee were changed) was used for this industrial problem.

4.6.1 Settings and Further Explanations of the Experiment

To simplify the situation, the tests here were based on simulation of unpaced flow lines [72], which were built by n stations with $n - 1$ inter-station buffers with only one machine for each station. The unpaced flow line does not mean that the simulator jumps between stations within the line as fast as possible during simulation, but means that a series of work stations with their tasks decoupled from each other by some methods, like buffers. In an unpaced flow line, the stations are operated independently except that the work delay of a station is caused by a storage shortage in its preceding buffer or a full buffer storage in its following buffer, and it is assumed that there are always parts available for the first station and the parts can be always shipped out in the last station [73]. Figure 4.3 is an example model of an unpaced flow line with 6 stations and 5 buffers defined in FACTS Analyzer. [74]

Figure 4.3: A simple FACTS simulation model of an unpaced flow line with 6 workstations and 5 buffers

The provided Application Programming Interface of FACTS Analyzer is able to provide the user with the Throughput, WIP and LT information of the unpaced flow line for each unique settings of the buffers and machines. For the example model in Figure 4.3, when setting the process time of M3 to 30 seconds and the rest to 27 seconds, the availability of M1 to M6 to 95%, and all the buffer sizes to 10, then the simulation returned Throughput 103.41, WIP 24.90, and LT 866.76.

Simulations in FACTS Analyzer are carried out in a replication style for each evaluation. The simulation engine will simulate a specified number of replication times for a setting to have multiple values for each output variable, and then return the averaged value for each. The replication were all set into 5 for the tests in this project, thus using the final output of WIP in 24.90 as an example, it was the average of 5 WIPs obtained by simulating the model 5 times.

FACTS Analyzer plays the role as an oracle here in the context of Active Learning and is able to provide response values for every requested experiment. Using a standard laptop computer, it took approximately 3.6 to 12.7 seconds to simulate one requested experiment (one set of parameter values) 5 times (the specified replication) to report the 3 response values Throughput, WIP and LT.

For the following tests, all the buffer capacities were fixed at 10, and the main aim was to maximize the Throughput of the line by optimizing (tuning) the process time (in seconds) and availability (in percentage) of each station/machine in the production line. Therefore when there were n stations in the line, there were $2n$ independent (discrete) variables, and if each variable had M alternative values, then the size of the search space would be in M^{2n}.

QBC will need to calculate and compare the EIs for all the candidates in the search space, if use it as in the previous comparison experiments. But for complex model with a large search space, processing all candidates would be infeasible. Moreover, since the simulation time needed by FACTS Analyzer (querying labels from it) is substantial, it is impossible to investigate all possible experiments when the whole search space is large (for example 2^{18}). This difficulty leads to using QBC in combination with PSO. More specifically, here PSO is used to find the most promising experiment x that gives the most promising expected improvement $EI(x)$ while avoiding calculating $EI(x)$ for all values of x.

In order to test the implemented alternative approach in different scenarios, unpaced flow line with 6, 9 and 12 stations were used. Since FACTS Analyzer runs NSGA-II for optimization iteratively as well, the number of predictions/iterations/evaluations needed to find an acceptable x_next for the function minimum could be directly compared with the Active Learning approach in as a performance criterion.

4.6.2 Unpaced Flow Line with 6 Stations

In this test case, the settings of process time and availability of each machine were limited to the choices in Table 4.10.

	M1	M2	M3	M4	M5	M6
Process Time	{27, 30}	{27, 30}	{27, 30}	{27, 30}	{27, 30}	{27, 30}
Availability	{95, 98}	{95, 98}	{95, 98}	{95, 98}	{95, 98}	{95, 98}

Table 4.10: Choices of process time and availability for the 6 machines in the line

Since there are 6 stations ($n = 6$), 2 independent variables (Process Time and Availability) for each station, and 2 value options ($M = 2$) for each variable, the search space here had $4096 (= 2^{2 \times 6})$ unique alternatives. The method for the test here was first to use FACTS Analyzer to find out all the response values for all these alternatives (candidate experiments), and then to randomly select 10 candidate experiments (that are not equal to the desired global optimum) as training data for the models in the committee of QBC to make prediction of x_next. This operation made all response values available before query, and made it possible and easy to check whether the optimum point found by QBC was the global minimum or not.

Table 4.11 contains some information about 17 predictions, the optimum was reached at the 8th prediction. This optimal settings should be the optimum solution in the given search space, and simulation results from FACTS Analyzer also suggest it. When taking the initial 10 training points into account as well, QBC totally took 18 iterations to gain the optimum. When instead using the optimization functionality in FACTS Analyzer, this optimum was gained at 171st evaluation as shown in the Figure 4.4. With considering the replication (in 5) settig for FACTS and population size (in 50) of NSGA-II, the simulation engine ran 90(= 18 × 5) times for QBC, and ran around 42750 (= 171 × 50 × 5) for NSGA-II.

The tests were also performed with initializing by 25, 50, 100, and 200 training instances for QBC, but all of them found the optimum at the first evaluation.

No.	Process Time and Avalability of M1 to M6	EI	-1*Throughput
Pred 1	27, 30, 27, 30, 27, 27, 98, 98, 98, 98, 98, 95	0.00116	-110.79
Pred 2	27, 30, 30, 30, 27, 27, 98, 98, 98, 98, 98, 98	0.02467	-111.96
Pred 3	27, 27, 30, 30, 27, 27, 98, 98, 98, 98, 98, 98	0.00054	-112.53
Pred 4	27, 27, 30, 30, 27, 27, 95, 98, 98, 98, 98, 98	3.08987e-09	-110.94
Pred 5	27, 27, 27, 30, 27, 27, 98, 98, 98, 98, 98, 98	6.67657e-10	-113.35
Pred 6	27, 27, 27, 30, 30, 27, 98, 98, 98, 98, 98, 98	5.91154e-08	-112.74
Pred 7	27, 27, 27, 30, 27, 30, 98, 98, 98, 98, 98, 98	7.36503e-17	-112.66
Pred 8	27, 27, 27, 27, 27, 27, 98, 98, 98, 98, 98, 98	1.28887e-23	**−123.03**
Pred 9	27, 27, 27, 27, 27, 30, 98, 98, 98, 98, 98, 98	2.55015e-07	-114.49
Pred 10	27, 27, 27, 27, 30, 27, 98, 98, 98, 98, 98, 98	4.02359e-22	-113.6
Pred 11	30, 30, 27, 30, 30, 30, 95, 95, 98, 95, 95, 95	2.98752e-16	-101.35
Pred 12	27, 27, 27, 27, 27, 27, 98, 98, 98, 98, 98, 95	1.51650e-18	-120.44
Pred 13	27, 27, 27, 27, 27, 27, 98, 95, 98, 98, 98, 98	2.78196e-28	-119.96
Pred 14	27, 27, 30, 27, 27, 27, 98, 98, 98, 98, 98, 98	2.74904e-31	-113.24
Pred 15	30, 27, 30, 30, 30, 30, 98, 98, 95, 98, 98, 95	1.13718e-33	-106.49
Pred 16	27, 27, 30, 27, 27, 30, 98, 98, 98, 98, 98, 98	2.59475e-38	-112.31
Pred 17	27, 27, 30, 30, 27, 30, 98, 98, 98, 98, 98, 98	7.37505e-48	-111.93

Table 4.11: Predictions of settings to gain the maximum of Throughput by QBC

4.6.3 Unpaced Flow Line with 9 Stations

Table 4.12 contains the setting choices for the unpaced flow line with 9 machines, and the size of the search space was $262144 (= 2^{2 \times 9})$ now since there are 9 stations ($n = 9$), 2 independent variables (Process Time and Availability) for each station, and 2 value options ($M = 2$) for each variable. Using FACTS Analyzer to obtain the 3 response values for each point in the search space was too time consuming since it took 3.6 to 12.7 seconds to process a single point. Therefore, the design of the experiment here was first to randomly select 500 instances from the search space, then to use FACTS Analyzer to obtain all responses (results) for these 500 points, and then to choose a desired number (≤ 500) of points from the labeled data as the training data set to train the models in

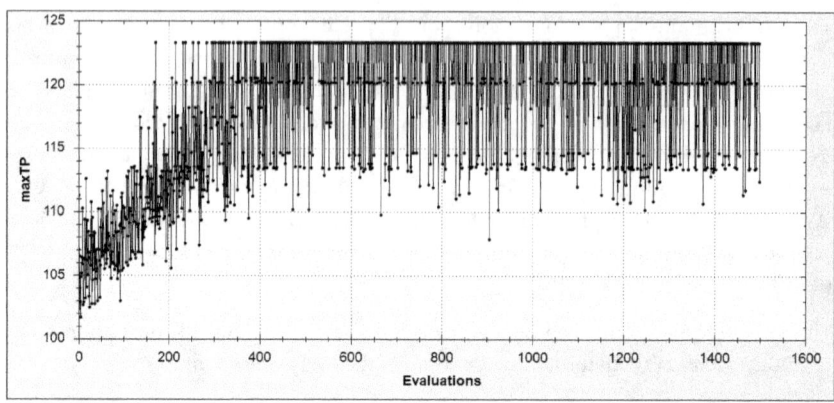

Figure 4.4: Simulation optimization of unpaced flow line with 6 stations in FACTS

the committee for predicting and evaluating the label information of all instance in the search space to find the promising optimum x_next.

In this test, 20 labeled instances were randomly selected to initialize the QBC, and the maximum Throughput in 107.79 was gained with the process time and availability settings for M1 to M9 as 27, 31.5, 27, 27, 27, 27, 27, 27, 27, 98, 98, 98, 98, 98, 98, 98, 94.6, 98 at the 15th evaluation. This optimum solution was the same as that from the simulation optimization by FACTS Analyzer, which was first found at its 615th evaluation as shown in Figure 4.5. With considering the replication (in 5) setting for FACTS and population size (in 50) of NSGA-II, the simulation engine ran $165 (= (20 + 15) \times 5)$ times for QBC, and ran around $153750 (= 615 \times 50 \times 5)$ for NSGA-II.

	M1	M2	M3	M4	M5	M6
Process Time	{27, 30}	{31.5, 35}	{27, 30}	{27, 30}	{27, 30}	{27, 30}
Availability	{95, 98}	{95, 98}	{95, 98}	{95, 98}	{95, 98}	{95, 98}
	M7	M8	M9			
Process Time	{27, 30}	{27, 30}	{27, 30}			
Availability	{95, 98}	{86, 94.6}	{95, 98}			

Table 4.12: Choices of process time and availability for the 9 machines in the line

Simplified multi-objective optimization using a single objective function was also attempted by using QBC. Except maximizing the Throughput, minimizing the WIP and LT were considered at the same time. The process of the test was almost the same as maximizing Throughput in last one, but except those: (i) when maximizing the Throughput, only the Throughput information was needed to train the models in the committee, now the three information including Throughput, WIP and LT was needed. The output dimension of a model is changed from one into three. (ii) Previously the EI was performed exclusively on Throughput in $EI(Throughput|D)$, but now it was calculated from a

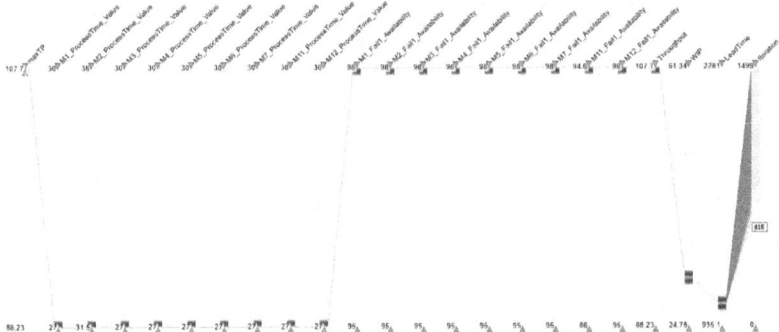

Figure 4.5: Simulation optimization of unpaced flow line with 9 stations in FACTS

weighted sum of the three responses Throughput, WIP and LT in $EI(MOP\_QBC|D)$. Here D is the observation instances (training data set), and $Throughput$ is from Equation 4.2, and MOP_QBC defined as follows

$$MOP\_QBC = w_1 \cdot Throughput + w_2 \cdot WIP + w_3 \cdot LT \qquad (4.5)$$

with $Throughput$, WIP and LT from Equation 4.2 to 4.4, and w_1, w_2 and w_3 in $-0.01, 0.02$, and 0.000625 respectively. The weights were selected according to user experience and the simulation results from FACTS Analyzer with intention to scale them near to -1 or 1 to have a same influence when calculating the expected improvement $EI(MOP\_QBC|D)$.

The multi-objective optimization test was initialized with 30 training data points and performed 30 optimization evaluations, and it was also carried out in FACTS Analyzer with 1500 evaluations by NSGA-II. The running results form the two methods are illustrated in Figure 4.6. Hypervolume is used as the performance indicator to compare the multi-objective optimization results from QBC and FACTS, which calculates the area or volume of a set of dominated solutions respected to a reference point. In this test. The reference point was selected as Throughput in 80, WIP in 65, and LT in 2400 in this test, and Figure 4.7 contains the Hypervolume score after each evaluation in QBC and FACTS. Although the score from FACTS (11.16×10^5 after 30 evaluations and 15.41×10^5 after 1500 evaluations) was higher than QBC (8.85×10^5 after 30 evaluations), the optimization results provided by QBC in LT and WIP were not bad, since they both reached to the level of minimum found by FACTS. While for Throughput, it was not equally promising since the found maximum was less than 97, while the optimum one in FACTS was over 107.

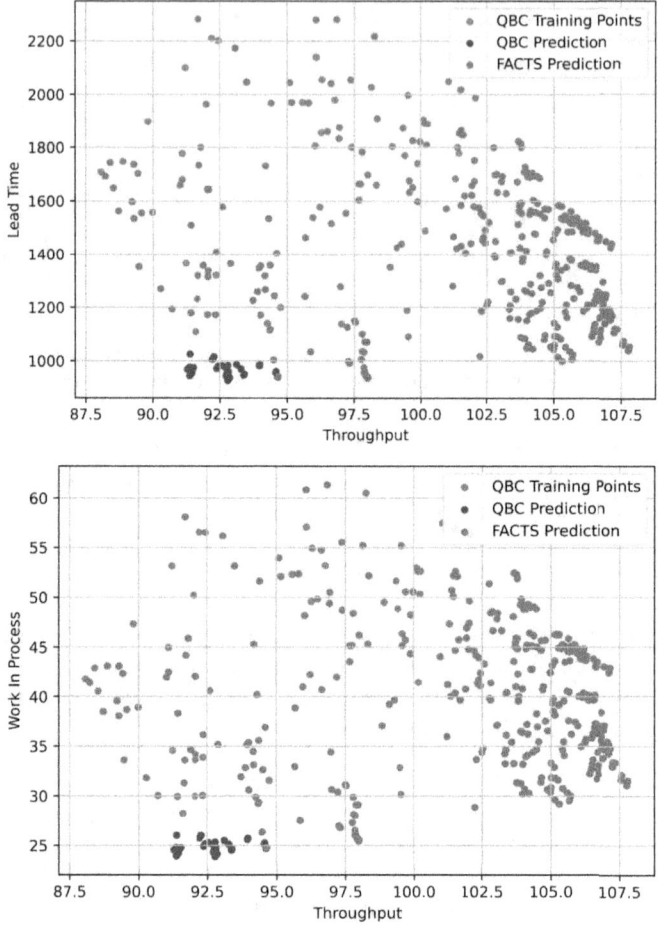

Figure 4.6: Throughput-LT (top) and Throughput-WIP (bottom) optimization by QBC and FACTS

4.6.4 Unpaced Flow Line with 12 Stations

Table 4.12 contained the setting choices for the unpaced flow line with 12 stations, and the size of the search space was $16777216 (= 2^{2 \times 12})$ now since there are 12 stations ($n = 12$), 2 independent variables (Process Time and Availability) for each station, and 2 value options ($M = 2$) for each variable. In this case, using the API of FACTS Analyzer to obtain all the response values was not feasible, and using models from the committee in QBC to evaluate all the instances in the search space was also difficult within a limited computation resource and time. Thus, the conventional way of QBC used in the

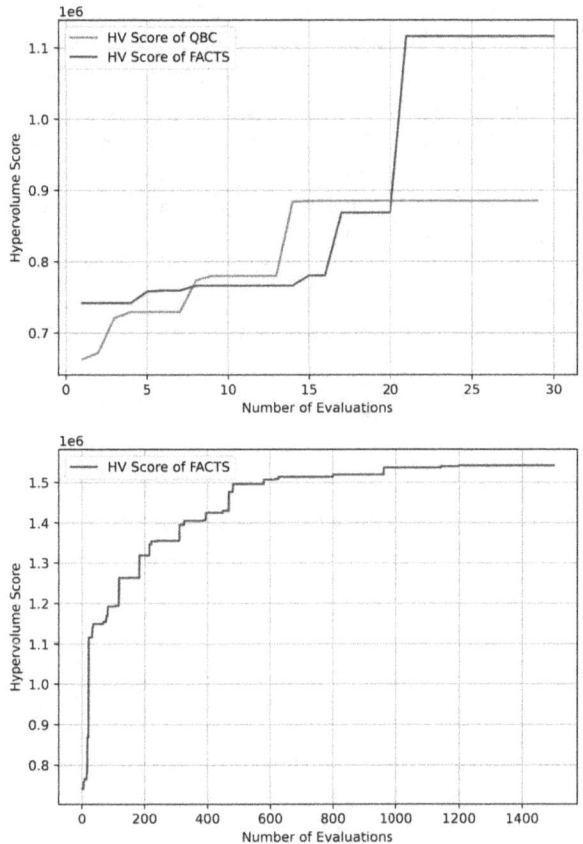

Figure 4.7: Hypervolume score in different evaluations by QBC & FACTS (top) and FACTS (bottom)

comparison experiments, which first evaluated the EI of all the candidates in the search space and then to find out the maximum one, cannot work here, so it was time for the designed PSO prediction method in QBC to play, in which the PSO method was only employed to find out the maximum EI from the search space.

	M1	M2	M3	M4	M5	M6
Process Time	{27, 30}	{31.5, 35}	{27, 30}	{27, 30}	{27, 30}	{27, 30}
Availability	{95, 98}	{95, 98}	{95, 98}	{95, 98}	{95, 98}	{95, 98}
	M7	M8	M9	M10	M11	M12
Process Time	{27, 30}	{27, 30}	{27, 30}	{27, 30}	{27, 30}	{27, 30}
Availability	{95, 98}	{95, 98}	{95, 98}	{95, 98}	{86, 94.6}	{95, 98}

Table 4.13: Choices of process time and availability for the 12 machines in the line

Based on the design principle described in section 3.4, the search space was defined in an array with 24 variables with each one being a continuous variable for PSO. It meant that the process time, M1 for example, originally was restricted to only be 27 or 30, but here it was able to be any real value between 27 and 30. Thus, in this experiment, the search spaces of FACTS Analyzer (discrete points) and QBC method (a continuous space) were different. QBC was initialized with 50 training data points to runs 50 evaluation to obtain the maximum response value of Throughput, and optimum value was 105.59 at the 15th evaluation by setting the Process Time and Availability of M1 to M12 to the following values: 28.35, 31.62, 27.36, 27.39, 27.44, 27.19, 27.12, 27.15, 28.15, 27.61, 28.56, 27.08, 97.86, 97.94, 97.8, 97.65, 97.38, 97.83, 96.69, 97.62, 97.62, 97.97, 94.17, and 97.64. While the optimum found by FACTS Analyzer was 107.8 at the 551st evaluation with the related settings 27, 31.5, 27, 27, 27, 27, 27, 27, 27, 27, 27, 27, 98, 98, 98, 98, 98, 98, 98, 98, 98, 98, 94.6, and 98.

5 Analysis and Discussion

There are four sections in this chapter. Section 5.1 relates to the first research question (How to use other machine learning methods other than GPs based regression within Active Learning framework to solve the global optimization problems for unknown objective functions?). Section 5.2 is correlated to the second research question (What is the performance of the investigated method compared with the classic GPs based regression over different type of functions and problems?). Section 5.3 contains the reflections of applying the investigated method into manufacturing simulation and optimization scenario, and Section 5.4 introduces the potential future work.

5.1 Toolbox Design and Implementation

5.1.1 Models in Committee

The basic idea in this project is to use uncertainty information, which comes from analysing the response values predicted by committee members of each candidate, to find the next most promising candidate towards finding the global optimum. Models in the committee play a key role for gaining the uncertainty information. Therefore, several machine learning models were presented and employed as committee members for QBC.

For the diversity of the committee members, the committee is only formed by one type of model, FNN, RT or GP models, for the experiments. Mixing different types of the models is an obvious and easy way to increase the diversity of the committee, but it was not tried due to lack of time and the fact that there is no simple and obvious way to quantify the diversities.

When using FNN to build the committee for QBC, two key parameters for defining the model were the number of hidden layers and the number of neurons in each hidden layer. In section 3.1.1, an idea was presented to employ multiple FNN models with each one having its number of layers equal to its numerical order in the committee and having the minimum number of neurons required in each layer to just fit the given training data. The resulting neural net models become diverse to some extent. However, plots from these models show that they are still quite similar. The proper number to maximize the performance is not clear, and this is the reason the FNN used in the comparison experiment are specified randomly instead to create more diversity.

Analysis and Discussion 57

For regression trees, three different methods in total are implemented in the toolbox (section 3.1.2). However one concern is that all the predicted values from the committee are not able to exceed the minimum and maximum of the label value in training data set. This means the mean and variance of an input x of interest are limited. Moreover, the piece-wise prediction performance from tree models makes EIs also piece-wise, and there are chances that the EIs for candidates within a certain range are all zero, which occurs when all RT models in the panel have the same predictions in that range.

5.1.2 Stop Criteria and PSO Prediction Method

Other aspects that may influence of the design and performance of the toolbox are the prediction stop criteria and the implementation of PSO. When tests are performed with the artificial data, the optimum is known, thus a proper range of the function value or an estimated area of the optimum location can be assigned to stop the training of the models in the committee. But for practical problems, such information is usually unknown, and the general stop criterion used within the method used was the number of predictions.

The employed PSO is used when the optimization problem is in high dimensions and it is not feasible to evaluation every candidate. Its running time is hugely influenced by the specified swarm size and running epochs, and when there are 5000 particles to run 100 steps each, a single evaluation cannot be gained within 15 minutes by the current implementing style and computer hardware (standard laptop). Using multi-thread or multi-process hardware to implement the method will improve the performance.

5.2 Comparison Experiments

5.2.1 Designs of the Experiments

The purpose of using functions from 1D to 3D is to test the performance of the QBC approach over different problems. Unfortunately one cannot know if the selected 30 functions used for the comparisons are sufficiently representative or not. Moreover, one limitation is that there is no statistical significance analysis performed.

Considering the noise level, when increasing it from 0.05 to 0.2, the Not Known case of the results reduces sharply in all the comparison experiments. It means that the number of QBC and GP being not able to find a minimum at the same time is reduced. Thus, if evaluated in terms of being able to find the global optimum or not, all the approaches perform better when noise level increases. The assumed reason behind this is the employed policy of acceptable minimums, because when noise level increases, the range/number of acceptable minimums is also extended, which may make a same x_next prediction become an acceptable optimum point.

5.2.2 Experiment Conclusions and Assumed Reasons

QBC with any of the three-discussed committees (built by FNNs, RTs or GPs) and the related settings are valid to be used for active learning optimization since it performs better than the baseline of random guess method. When consider noise level is in 0.05 and 0.2 and EIs are using Normal distribution estimation, only QBC with ensembles of GP models outperform a single GP model. When noise level is in 0.05, QBC with any discussed committee performs no worse than a single GP model. When noise level is in 0.2, a single GP outperforms QBC. Using KDE for EI calculation lowers the performance of QBC built by GP models.

The employed machine learning algorithm as committee member all perform better than the random guess for prediction, and the ensembles of them in QBC reserve its validity and advantages by using wisdom from the crowds when optimization. Models from the committee are able to to be in different configurations, which increase the diversities of the committee and the prediction responses of a label.

When using FNNs or RTs to build committee for QBC, the current evaluation of a candidate cannot use the prediction responses from previous evaluations made by the committee for the same candidate. But when using the GPs based Bayesian Optimization, an element in the covariance matrix is updated consistently by fitting new training instance with using the most recent posterior distribution as prior. Moreover, by QBC methods, the number of prediction responses of an candidate is limited to the number of committee members when there is not enough models in the committee, this reduces the performance of QBC when using KDE to calculate EI.

When using GP models in all the experiments, the kernels within them were selected randomly from the common ones presented in Scikit-learn package, including the Constant Kernel, White Kernel, Radial-basis Function Kernel etc. The initial bonds and scales of the covariance functions for GPs were also assigned randomly, and the kernel hyper parameters were optimized by Scikit-learn itself during fitting process. The random selection of the kernel functions and the initializing parameters made the GPs in the committee or the committees in various tests different. Therefore, diversities were imported into the committee at the same time with preserving the advantages of GP model itself.

When comes to the good performance of GPs over data with high level noise, there is a hyper-parameter α (in Equation 2.3.2, also in the Gaussian Process Regressor from Scikit-learn) to influence the updating of covariance matrix for the distribution. Different values of α enable the model to handle data in different noise levels. When the value of α is set to the variance of the noise, then the GP model is fitted as using the interval policy presented in Section 3.2.1, but it will take more evaluations/steps to reach an acceptable minimum compared when setting α to a small value close to zero, since a larger α will result in a higher uncertainty on the prediction responses.

5.3 Application in Industrial Simulation Problem

For tests on the unpaced flow line with 6 and 9 stations, QBC use substantially less calls of the simulation engine compared with the simulation of FACTS Analyzer for reaching close to the global optimum. That means, if in real world experiments, QBC as an Active Learning approach will have advantages on using less practical experiments to reach a near optimum compared with optimizing with NSGA-II.

For the optimizing with QBC and simulation with the API of FACTS Analyzer, simulating a single unique setting of unpaced flow line with 6, 9, and 12 stations took around 7.83, 3.58 and 12.69 seconds respectively. It was strange that unpaced flow line with 9 stations took the least time, and the reason was unknown since the interaction between QBC with FACTS Analyzer API took many steps among Python, CMD of Windows, the API, reading and writing files on the disk. While for simulation and optimization by FACTS Analyzer, with setting evaluations to 1500, population to 50 and replication to 5, it took around 31, 35 and 45 minutes respectively for the unpaced flow line with 6, 9, and 12 stations, which meant that it took only $0.025\ (= 31 \times 60 \div 1500 \div 50)$ to $0.036\ (= 45 \times 60 \div 1500 \div 50)$ seconds to simulate one unique settings with 5 replications inside FACTS Analyzer. Therefore, the running time of QBC and FACTS Analyzer were not compared directly, and the simulation calls/times by the simulation engine were counted instead. Another interesting observation was that by increasing the number of training points for the models in committee of QBC, the fitting time of each model would increase significantly.

When running multiple objective optimization for maximizing Throughput, minimizing WIP and LT by QBC, the weights used for scaling the direct response information to -1, 1 and 1 are vital. The first test running was performed without any scaling, and then the optimization mainly focuses on the Lead Time part. The assumed reason is that the Lead Time being able to change in a wider range domains the reduction of their summation, since LT is able to be up to 1500, while Throughput and WIP can only be up to 150 and 100 respectively. But right now there is no good strategy to choose the weights, and other methods or hyper parameter values might be imported here for improvement.

For tests on the unpaced flow line with 12 stations, the results gained by QBC are close to each other, and the reason might be that it is trapped in a local minimum. Meanwhile, the settings of the test performed by QBC and FACTS have many differences. QBC runs 50 predictions (with 50 initializing training samples), while FACTS performs 1500 evaluations; Also, the size of the search domain for FACTS is 2^{24}, but it is infinite for QBC method, but this can be improved by further modifying the defining rule of search space. However the main purpose of this test is to check whether the PSO method within QBC is useful or not and the capability of applying QBC to high dimension problems.

5.4 Future Work

One feature of QBC is that when importing new labeled data into the training data set, the predictions for each candidate will be constructed again, and the predictions and associated models from the previous step for a candidate are all thrown away. When employing Gaussian Processes as surrogate models in the combination with Bayesian Inference, there is a prior and Bayes theorem linking the whole process, and normally a new training data point only causes local changes of the surrogate model. Therefore, introducing hyper parameters or other methods into QBC to further mimic the ideas of Bayesian Optimization using Gaussian Processes may lead to a better performance even using various models for building the committee.

Another feature of QBC is that the contributions of the different models in the committee to the final prediction are not weighted. When QBC has a committee built by FNN models, sometimes a committee member cannot fit the data after being trained for a long time even with increasing its number of neurons. To save the training time, weights related to training time and the final loss from evaluation criteria could be used to make such models less influential. The method of using and updating these weights has strong similarities with the idea of boosting.

6 Conclusion

A Query By Committee based alternative approach (QBC) to Active Learning for global optimization has been studied, and a computational toolbox has been built in Python in order to perform this scientific investigation. Different machine learning methods can be studied in terms of how uncertain their predictions are, and QBC with committees built on Feedforward Neural Network, Regression Tree and Gaussian Process models can be compared with the random guessing/selection of new experiments.

Comparisons were made when the Active Learning for optimization was done by means of Bayesian inference using Gaussian Processes as well as by means of QBC. In these studies, the goals were to find global minima of some 1D, 2D and 3D functions by using as few function evaluations as possible. The comparison results show that QBC with a committee of Gaussian Process models derived from the training data using Bayesian Inference outperforms a single Gaussian Process model for different noise levels. The results also showed that QBC with committees built by Feed Forward Neural Networks and Regression Trees do not outcompete the single Gaussian Process modelling approach. Finally it was also found that using Kernel Density Estimation lowered the performance compared to using the Normal distribution to estimate the probability density function needed for calculating the Expected Improvement under the setting used in the experiment.

The toolbox was also tested on industrial simulation optimization problems, and the results show its potentials of using less function evaluations to find the optimum and its capability of handling problems from low to high dimensions in close to realistic production scenarios.

Future research work are able to be performed along the direction of importing methods or hyper parameters into QBC to enable the reuse of predictions from previous evaluation stages by committee members, or the direction of importing different weights for models in committee.

www.ingramcontent.com/pod-product-compliance
Lightning Source LLC
LaVergne TN
LVHW020436080526
838202LV00055B/5217